Settling a Dispute

NEW TEXTS FROM ANCIENT CULTURES 1

Edited by

Traianos Gagos, University of Michigan
Ann Ellis Hanson, University of Michigan
Ludwig Koenen, University of Michigan
& Peter van Minnen, Duke University

Settling a Dispute

Toward a Legal Anthropology of Late Antique Egypt

Traianos Gagos & Peter van Minnen

Ann Arbor

THE UNIVERSITY OF MICHIGAN PRESS

Published in the United States of America by
The University of Michigan Press
♾ Printed on acid-free paper

1997 1996 1995 1994 4 3 2 1

Library of Congress Cataloging-in-Publication Data

Gagos, Traianos.
Settling a dispute : toward a legal anthropology of late antique Egypt / Traianos Gagos & Peter van Minnen.
p. cm. — (New texts from ancient cultures)
Includes a Greek text of a 6th century A.D. papyrus; with translation, commentaries, and introduction in English.
Includes bibliographical references and index.
ISBN 0-472-09590-0 (alk. paper). —— ISBN 0-472-06590-4 (pbk. : alk. paper)
1. Compromise (Roman law)—History—Sources. 2. Vendors and purchasers (Roman law))—History—Sources. 3. Liens (Roman law—History—Sources. 4. Compromise (Law—Aphrodito (Extinct city—History—Sources. 5. Vendors and purchasers—Aphrodito (Extinct city)—History—Sources. 6. Liens—Aphrodito (Extinct city)—History—Sources. I. Minnen, P. van. II. Title. III. Series.
KJA670.E3 1994
346.45'6350432—dc20
[344.563206432] 94-31945
CIP

Preface

There are various reasons for publishing a document from late antique Egypt as a separate monograph. Its content should appeal to scholars from a large number of disciplines, which makes it undesirable to bury it in a specialized journal of some sort–if we could ever find one that accepts articles of more than a hundred pages. We believe that by employing the strategies discussed in section 1 of our introduction we have made a small contribution towards creating a more sympathetic reading of late antique documents from Egypt, such as the one we publish here. We hope our work will encourage scholars and students interested in the world of late antiquity to take note of these documents and their context.

We would like to thank all the individuals and institutions that helped us turn our work into a real pleasure. Special thanks are due to Dr. Rosario Pintaudi, of Florence, who kindly supplied a photograph of the Vatican part of the document, the Special Collections Library at Ann Arbor, which gave us permission to publish the Michigan part of the document, the anonymous readers of the University of Michigan Press and Dr. Louise P. Smith, of Duke University, whose kind remarks have been very helpful to us, and Dr. Ellen Bauerle, Classics editor of the University of Michigan Press, who furthered our work with unfailing support.

We would like to dedicate this volume to Louise C. Youtie for her lifelong devotion to papyrology at the University of Michigan.

Ann Arbor, June 1994

Contents

Abbreviations

Abh. Gött.	Abhandlungen der Akademie der Wissenschaften in Göttingen. Phil.-Hist. Klasse, Third series
ANRW	*Aufstieg und Niedergang der Römischen Welt*
ASP	American Studies in Papyrology
Basilica	(i) *Basilicorum Libri LX*, edited by G.M. Heimbach (Leipzig, 1833-1870) (ii) *Basilicorum Libri* LX. Series A, Vols. 1-8; Series B, Vols. 1-9, edited by H.J. Scheltema a.o. (Groningen, 1953-1988)
BASP	*Bulletin of the American Society of Papyrologists*
BÉ	"Bulletin épigraphique," annual report in *Revue des Études Grecques*
Berichtigungsliste	*Berichtigungsliste der Griechischen Papyrusurkunden aus Ägypten.* 8 Vols., edited by F. Preisigke a.o. (Berlin, Heidelberg & Leiden, 1922-1992)
BKU	*Aegyptische Urkunden aus den koeniglichen Museen zu Berlin. Koptische Urkunden*
BSAC	*Bulletin de la Société d'Archéologie Copte*
CdÉ	*Chronique d'Égypte*
Cod.Just.	*Codex Justinianus*, Vol. 2 of *Corpus Juris Civilis*, edited by P. Krüger. 6th ed. (Berlin, 1895)
FF	*Forschungen und Fortschritte*
GRBS	*Greek, Roman, and Byzantine Studies*
HSCP	*Harvard Studies in Classical Philology*
JARCE	*Journal of the American Research Center in Egypt*
JHS	*Journal of Hellenic Studies*
JJP	*Journal of Juristic Papyrology*

JRA	*Journal of Roman Archaeology*
JRS	*Journal of Roman Studies*
MPER	Mitteilungen aus der Papyrussammlung der Österreichischen Nationalbibliothek in Wien, New Series
Münch. Beitr.	Münchener Beiträge zur Papyrusforschung und Antiken Rechtsgeschichte
Novellae	*Novellae*, Vol. 3 of *Corpus Juris Civilis*, edited by R. Schoell and W. Kroll. 2d ed. (Berlin, 1899)
Pap. Brux.	Papyrologica Bruxellensia
Pap. Colon.	Papyrologica Coloniensia
Pap. Flor.	Papyrologica Florentina
PCPhS	*Proceedings of the Cambridge Philological Society*
P.Köln ägypt.	*Kölner ägyptische Papyri*
P.Ryl. copt.	*Catalogue of the Coptic Manuscripts in the Collection of the John Rylands Library*, edited by W.E. Crum
RdÉ	*Revue d'Égyptologie*
RÉAug	*Revue des Études Augustiniennes*
RhM	*Rheinisches Museum*
RIDA	*Revue Internationale des Droits de l'Antiquité*
SAOC	Studies in Ancient Oriental Civilization
Stud. Pal.	Studien zur Palaeographie und Papyruskunde
T&M	*Travaux et Mémoires*
TAPA	*Transactions of the American Philological Association*
YCS	*Yale Classical Studies*
ZPE	*Zeitschrift für Papyrologie und Epigraphik*
ZSS	*Zeitschrift der Savigny-Stiftung*, Romanistische Abteilung

Introduction

1. *What this book is all about*

In this monograph we publish the text of a long and important document from late antiquity written on papyrus, provide an exhaustive commentary on the text, and give enough background information to satisfy the needs of modern readers.

Papyrus documents from late antiquity were published in large quantities in the early days of papyrology. Unfortunately, a method of publication current in those times has rendered most of these early editions, especially of papyri from the collections in Cairo, Florence, and London,[1] virtually inaccessible to the majority of scholars. With few exceptions, such as the edition of papyri from the Munich collection (*P.München.* I) and E. von Druffel's monograph on the Heidelberg papyrus with the inventory number 311,[2] the early publications present the texts with little help to the reader. Apart from giving short introductory remarks and a few notes, the editors print the texts as they are found on the papyri. Frequent abbreviations are not resolved, no accents are added

---

1 Among papyrologists, for the sake of brevity, the editions of these texts are known as *P.Cair.Masp.*, *P.Flor.*, and *P.Lond.* In this monograph we follow this convention and print such abbreviations of standard papyrus editions in italics. For full bibliographical information readers should consult J.F. Oates a.o., *Checklist of Editions of Greek and Latin Papyri, Ostraca and Tablets.* BASP, Supplements, Vol. 7 (4th ed., Atlanta, 1992).

2 E. von Druffel, *Papyrologische Studien zum byzantinischen Urkundenwesen im Anschluss an P. Heidelberg 311* (Munich, 1915).

to help the reader decide on ambiguous grammatical forms, and no translations are provided.[3] The present monograph cannot make up for this, but it should underscore the vital interest of these papyri for the study of late antiquity as well as the importance of reclaiming them for present-day scholarship.

In organizing our publication we have departed somewhat from current editorial practice. We start, not with the traditional transcription of the Greek text, as it is found on the papyrus, but with a normalized version of the text (the reading text) and an English translation on facing pages. In the "normalization" process, we have not intervened in the syntax or the word order of the text, as this would have resulted in an artificial construct based on our view of stylistic correctness. We have limited our intervention to matters of orthography and slips of the pen, such as in line 89. Few changes of this kind were necessary, because the papyrus is well preserved and the text was written by an educated scribe. We have, however, divided both the reading text and the translation into paragraphs as a modern printed text should be to assist readers who might be interested in the content of the document rather than in strictly textual matters. In other words, we have arranged the reading text according to the structure of the document rather than the line divisions on the papyrus, although we have marked these line divisions in the text (by inserting |) for ease of reference. We hope that our arrangement will enhance the accessibility of our material for a wide spectrum of scholars interested in late antiquity. In the reading text we have also removed the diacritics and conventions that are customary in papyrological editions, which we explain on p. 65, preceding the transcription of the Greek text. Consequently, the reading text does not distinguish between the actual text as found on the papyrus and our supplements and corrections –however few these may be. For the sake of accuracy readers familiar with papyrological lore are encouraged to refer to the transcription of the Greek text, which contains the text as produced by the scribe as well as all the diacritics and papyrological conventions.

In the introduction we provide the background needed to understand the document and all other information of general interest that would otherwise be lost in the commentary. First we present some pre-

---

3 The dismay caused by the inaccessibility of *P.Cair.Masp.* has led scholars to undertake, as of 1988, the republication of these invaluable texts in a modern form. For the announcement of this project see J.G. Keenan, "On the Cairo Maspero Papyri," *Proc. XIXth Int. Congr. Papyr.* Vol. 1 (Cairo, 1992) 85-94.

liminary remarks about the study of late antique Egypt and its rich data base, of which our document is but a tiny part (sections 2-4). Next we discuss the content of the text in more detail in the form of both a discussion of the case and an outline of the text (sections 5-7). Then we proceed to the wider background relating to the case (sections 8-10). Many of the statements in the introduction are based on the more extensive argumentation and full documentation found in the commentary, which presents yet another level of approach to the text. The discussion there is detailed and more specialized. Individual notes, depending on their function, may contain several quotations from parallel Greek documents or more detailed bibliographical references.

The document records the settlement of a dispute over a piece of property near the ancient village of Aphrodito in Upper Egypt[4] in about A.D. 537. The text was written by a professional scribe on a long roll of papyrus (about 30 cm wide and 180 cm long). The largest portion of the papyrus found its way to the United States some fifty years ago and now bears the inventory number 6922 in the papyrus collection at the University of Michigan in Ann Arbor. It entered this collection in 1946 as a gift from the late Professor Campbell Bonner. In the inventory it is listed as a single acquisition, unrelated to the other papyri from Aphrodito, which were purchased for the collection a few years earlier in 1943 and mostly published by P.J. Sijpesteijn in 1977.[5] Nothing more is known about the origin of P.Mich.inv. 6922 and these other papyri.[6] The Michigan piece is in an excellent state of preservation and retains some of its original flexibility. Taken out of its modern frame it curls up if exposed to the light of a bright lamp. When we first discovered the Michigan papyrus we quickly established that it was the lower part of a fragment in the Vatican library that had been published by R. Pintaudi in

4 For the location of towns in late antique Egypt, see the map on p. 129.

5 P.J. Sijpesteijn, *The Aphrodite Papyri in the University of Michigan Papyrus Collection* (Zutphen, 1977), also known as *P.Mich.* XIII. See the thorough review by J. Gascou, *CdÉ* 52 (1977): 360-68. In addition to some unpublished fragments of Greek documents from Aphrodito the Michigan collection still holds one long unpublished Coptic document, a contract of exchange of property (P.Mich. inv. 6898). For the variable spelling of the name of the village as Aphrodite and Aphrodito and the spelling we adopt in this monograph see below, note 25.

6 We have not been able to establish whether our papyrus and those in *P.Mich.* XIII belong to the same find. See *P.Mich.* XIII, p. ix and *P.Vat.Aphrod.*, p. 5.

1980.[7] P.Mich.inv. 6922 preserves the lower traces of line 24 of *P.Vat.Aphrod.* 10 and continues for another ninety-two lines. Put together, the two pieces give us an almost complete text except for the dating formula at the top. The signatures at the bottom of the Michigan section show that the papyrus is virtually complete there. A reexamination of the plate of *P.Vat.Aphrod.* 10 enabled us to improve the transcription of the first editor. We republish the Vatican fragment here with his permission.

2. *Late antique Egypt*

The study of late antiquity from the fourth to the seventh century A.D. has attracted the attention of a growing number of scholars in the past twenty years. Late antiquity is indeed an attractive field of study, because its society was in many ways comparable to our own. Scholars have always stressed the ever-growing bureaucracy and the increasing importance of professional services in the economy of late antiquity as developments parallel to what was going on in their own society.[8] However, growing inefficiency in government and a decline in the economy as a whole seem particularly apt parallels to our day and age. In late antiquity the public response to the problems facing the Roman empire was unable to prevent its fall.

Late antiquity is also an attractive field of study because its society was in some ways strikingly different from our own. The insistence on theological correctness, the prominent role of the holy men and women in society,[9] the careful use of expressions and titles of respect when people addressed one another, and the formal hierarchy in all walks of life are unfamiliar to us. Yet in a time of rapid change the study of civilizations with roots radically different from ours can provide an interesting form of reorientation. And a multicultural society that somehow managed to survive for centuries on principles we no longer share presents something of a challenge.

---

7 R. Pintaudi, *I papiri vaticani greci di Aphrodito* (Vatican City, 1980), also known as *P.Vat.Aphrod.* See the review by J. Gascou, *Aegyptus* 61 (1981): 274-81.

8 See, e.g., A.H.M. Jones, *The Later Roman Empire: A Social, Economic and Administrative Survey*, 3 Vols. (Oxford, 1964).

9 See, e.g., P. Brown, *Society and the Holy in Late Antiquity, A.D. 150-750* (Berkeley, 1982).

Late antique Egypt was an integral part of the later Roman empire.[10] In the earlier Roman empire the country was kept separate from the rest of the Mediterranean world for political reasons and in a variety of ways. This was no longer the case in late antiquity. Administrative institutions in late antique Egypt down to the lowest level of government were very similar to those elsewhere in the Roman world. This situation was to a large degree due to the emperor Diocletian and his colleagues and to their immediate successors, whose aim was to unify and simplify the administrative system in an effort to consolidate the empire. The closed currency system of Egypt, which separated its economy from that of other countries under the early Roman emperors, was abolished by Diocletian and replaced by a universal currency system based on the solidus.[11] From the conquest of Egypt by Augustus until the time of Diocletian, Egypt had had its own currency based on the tetradrachm and it was not permitted to take Egyptian money out of the country. It is unlikely that the gold and silver coins found in Egyptian hoards but issued elsewhere were ever part of the ordinary currency used in Egypt.

Religion had also set Egypt apart from other countries throughout antiquity. Ancient Egyptian religion was characterized on the one hand by its exotic array of zoomorphic gods and on the other hand by the omnipresence of its very business-like priests. In the early Roman empire the Egyptian gods Isis and Serapis were very popular elsewhere in the Mediterranean world, but they were anthropomorphic gods and could not conceal the fact that what was going on in Egyptian religion in general was as strange as ever.[12] In the fourth century all this had finally started to give way to a new faith, Christianity, which Egypt was to share with the rest of the empire. That the church in Egypt by and large came to adhere to doctrines different from those elsewhere in no way interferes with this fundamental fact. The isolation of a "Coptic" church, i.e., the so-called monophysite Christians of Egypt, is a byproduct of the conquest of Egypt by the Arabs in the mid-seventh century.

---

10 See for this, e.g., H.I. Bell, *Egypt from Alexander the Great to the Arab Conquest* (Oxford, 1948) 101-34.

11 See L.C. West & A.C. Johnson, *Currency in Roman and Byzantine Egypt* (Princeton, 1944), especially pp. 1 and 97.

12 See K.A.D. Smelik & E.A. Hemelrijk, "'Who Knows Not What Monsters Demented Egypt Worships? Opinions on Egyptian Animal Worship in Antiquity as Part of the Ancient Conception of Egypt," *ANRW* II 17.4 (1984): 1852-2000.

Scholarship particularly devoted to late antique Egypt follows the main lines set out for late antiquity in general.[13] During the early part of this century much attention was devoted to the military, administrative, and legal history of late antique Egypt. The sharp increase in publications of late antique documents written on papyrus seemed to warrant this particular version of historical interest. Scholars such as J. Maspero and H.I. Bell contributed heavily to the study of late antique Egypt through their text publications (*P.Cair.Masp.* and *P.Lond.* respectively). Others contributed studies on the administration (M. Gelzer and G. Rouillard)[14] and the development of the so-called large estate as a feature of economic history (E.R. Hardy).[15] These studies are indispensable to students of late antique Egypt, but their revision is long overdue.

The study of late antique Egypt was revived in the last thirty years by scholars interested in the broader spectrum of social and economic history. New methods and strategies have been employed, but modern scholarship could not exist without the work of a previous generation of scholars. There has been a large number of publications on specific aspects of late antique Egypt, such as administration, agricultural growth and decline, religion, and the growth of the church as an institution of social and economic power.[16] Many of these works are mentioned in our commentary. Here we note only those scholars whose work deals with broader issues. R. Rémondon started publishing studies on late antique Egypt in the fifties[17] and I.F. Fikhman did so in the sixties.[18] The

---

13 For details, see J.G. Keenan, "Papyrology and Byzantine Historiography," *Alpha to Omega: Studies in Honor of George John Szemler* (Chicago, 1993): 111-22.

14 M. Gelzer, *Studien zur byzantinischen Verwaltung Ägyptens* (Leipzig, 1909) and G. Rouillard, *L'administration civile de l'Égypte byzantine* (2d ed. Paris, 1928).

15 E.R. Hardy, *The Large Estates of Byzantine Egypt* (New York, 1931).

16 See, e.g., E. Wipszycka, *Les ressources et les activités économiques des églises en Égypte du IVe au VIIIe siècle* (Brussels, 1972).

17 See the posthumously published summary in R. Rémondon, "Les contradictions de la société égyptienne à l'époque byzantine," *JJP* 18 (1974): 17-32.

18 I.F. Fikhman, *Egipet na rubezhe dvukh epokh. Remeslenniki i remeslennyi trud v IV - seredine VII v.* (Moscow, 1965), on the craftsmen in late antique Egypt, and *Oksirinkh – gorod papirusov* (Moscow & Leningrad, 1976). The latter contains a summary in French. A number of articles in English, French, and German sum-

general inaccessibility of Fikhman's major studies–*Rossica non leguntur*–is hardly his fault, but it adds not a little to the difficulties facing the modern historian of late antique Egypt. Like the major text editions of late antique documents on papyrus, Fikhman's studies are at once indispensable and intractable. J.G. Keenan made his début with studies on late antique Egypt in the seventies,[19] and L.S.B. MacCoull followed in the eighties.[20] The themes they broached in a series of articles and one monograph show the potential and the diverse character of the material from late antique Egypt. Their studies cover a wide range of topics, such as expressions of social status in nomenclature and titulature, social mobility, the impact of legislation on the day-to-day workings of society, the ownership of land and its exploitation, the dynamics of the relations between city and countryside, and the cultural heritage shared by the educated inhabitants of Egypt with those in the rest of the empire. R.S. Bagnall has recently joined their ranks with another monograph on the period up to middle of the fifth century.[21] J. Gascou is expected to follow soon with the publication of an extensive tax list.[22]

Today students of late antique Egypt have come to realize that the data base for their field of study is unique in many ways. Our contribution to the subject is modest. In the notes on the first lines (1a-5) we have paid special attention to details that are often passed over in silence elsewhere: the painstaking use of the correct titles and status designations in documents from late antiquity and the central role of Antinoopolis within the administration of late antique Egypt. Antinoopolis was founded by the emperor Hadrian and had become the capital of the province of the Lower Thebais (roughly corresponding to the upper part of the southern half of Egypt). The city undoubtedly attracted many businessmen, scholars, poets and other performers, and it also accommodated a steady stream of those who had some legal affair to settle, because the major courts in the Lower Thebais were located in Antinoopolis. As is clear from our text the occasional visitor from another place could also turn into a permanent resident, perhaps

---

marize Fikhman's major studies, but a wealth of detail goes by and large unnoticed.

19 See, e.g., J.G. Keenan, "On Law and Society in Late Roman Egypt," *ZPE* 17 (1975): 237-50.

20 Culminating in her *Dioscorus of Aphrodito: His Work and His World* (Berkeley, 1988).

21 R.S. Bagnall, *Egypt in Late Antiquity* (Princeton, 1993).

22 The publication of *P.Sorb.* II is imminent.

attracted by the monumental beauty of the many public buildings in Antinoopolis, which is called a "fair city" in line 1 of our text, or by the opportunities the city offered for living the good life.

3. *Late antique Aphrodito*

The main source of information for late antique Egypt are documentary papyri that have been preserved in the ruins of ancient towns. The major cities that provided the bulk of the papyri from the Ptolemaic and earlier Roman periods do so for the later Roman period as well: Arsinoe and Heracleopolis for the Ptolemaic period, Arsinoe, Oxyrhynchus and Hermopolis for the earlier Roman period. There are, however, important differences. Whereas the earlier Roman papyri from Arsinoe were supplemented to a large extent by papyri from the countryside around Arsinoe (commonly known as the Fayyum), the villages that yielded these papyri virtually dried up as a source in the later Roman period. Villages like Theadelphia and Karanis may well have literally dried up when the water from the Nile no longer reached them. They were located at the end of a long trajectory of irrigation channels right on the edge of the inhospitable desert, which contributed its part to the decline of the complex irrigation system and the gradual decline of the village communities. Villages located in the Nile valley itself are generally not an important source of papyri. In the late antique period there is one exception to this rule: Aphrodito.[23]

Accidental finds at the site of ancient Aphrodito in 1901, monitored excavations in 1905, and clandestine diggings in the late thirties[24] yielded an enormous mass of documentary and some literary papyri. The finds were dispersed over a good number of institutions throughout the world. Late antique papyri from Aphrodito are now kept in the major libraries in Europe and the United States as well as in Cairo and Alexandria. They date either from the reigns of Justinian (A.D. 527-65) and Justin II (565-78) or from the early Arab period (early eighth century A.D.). Apparently the papers of two public figures from late antique Aphrodito were found. The later group consists mainly of administrative

23 The following is based mainly on H.I. Bell, "An Egyptian Village in the Age of Justinian," *JHAS* 64 (1944): 21-36 and J.G. Keenan, "The Aphrodito Papyri and Village Life in Byzantine Egypt," *BSAC* 26 (1984): 51-63.

24 See the detailed discussion by L.S.B. MacCoull, op. cit. (note 20 above) 2-5.

documents from the office of a certain Qorrah ibn Sharik. The earlier group from the reigns of Justinian and Justin II is more diversified and contains many notarial documents. In this introduction we will concentrate on this earlier group of documents, which deals mainly with private transactions among villagers of Aphrodito.

Most papyri from sixth-century Aphrodito[25] refer to the village's most prominent family, the descendants of Psimanobet and his son Dioscorus (see the family tree on p. 131). The male members of this family served as leaders of their community in successive generations and represented the village in its dealings with both the local authorities and the imperial family in Constantinople. Because they were respected for their wealth and literacy, which were exceptional at least by village standards, they often drafted documents on behalf of their fellow villagers or signed documents for illiterates who could not do it themselves. Frequently they were called upon to append their signatures as witnesses to contracts, or they were asked to keep the papers of others. Thus the family's archive came to contain not only their personal papers, but also documents and drafts of documents relating to the affairs of neighbors and friends. Eventually all these texts ended up with Dioscorus, son of Apollos, the man best known to us from this family, and it is through Dioscorus' eyes that we recapture the most vivid glimpses of life in late antique Aphrodito. Dioscorus himself will be the subject of our next section, but we sketch first in outline his Aphrodito, a bustling and populous village.

Although Aphrodito was technically styled a village in late antiquity, it must have been a town of considerable size, because in earlier periods it had been the capital of a small district of its own, known as the Aphroditopolite nome (Egypt was divided in about forty such "nomes" of various size). This district lost its independence when it was incorporated into the larger and neighboring Antaeopolite nome, but Aphrodito tried to stay independent from the new capital, Antaeopolis, as much as possible. When it came to paying taxes Aphrodito dealt with the government directly, without the intermediary of the nome capital. This independence in tax matters or *autopragia* seems to have been an ancient privilege preserved under the new regime in late antiquity. Yet some time during the sixth century Aphrodito exchanged its independent sta-

25 Strictly speaking the village was only called Aphrodito after the Arab conquest in the middle of the seventh century. We use this spelling rather than Aphrodite, because it is the traditional spelling. See L.S.B. MacCoull, op. cit. (note 20 above) 7, note 3.

tus for one of direct dependence on the house of the emperor, apparently through the emperor's wife, Theodora. The town requested this change to protect itself against the growing pressure from the more powerful nome capital Antaeopolis. This kind of protection is a form of patronage the doubtful benefits of which the less powerful in late antique Egypt coveted to protect themselves against their more powerful neighbors. Despite the presence of representatives of the imperial government in Egypt, the more direct pressure on Aphrodito from tax collectors in nearby Antaeopolis would have been hard to resist if there had been no effective counterpressure from Constantinople. And nothing could be more effective than direct envoys from the emperor himself. The inhabitants of Aphrodito tried their best to secure the support of the imperial family, and they sent a number of representatives to Constantinople carrying petitions to the emperor and the empress.

A long text requesting the help of the empress, in addition to providing information about the tax status of the village within the administrative structure of late antique Egypt, sheds light on the social structure of Aphrodito itself. This document is *P.Cair.Masp.* III 67283.[26] It was prepared in A.D. 547/548 on behalf of the inhabitants of Aphrodito and was entrusted to a number of deputies who had to present it to the empress Theodora in Constantinople in person. In the document the town as a collective informs the empress of the illegal dealings of the authorities in Antaeopolis, who want to subsume the town under their administrative jurisdiction. Indeed the village as a whole had a stake in the matter, because the responsibility to pay taxes rested with the landowners collectively. The text of the request was written by Dioscorus, son of Apollos, and signed by a large number of literate and some illiterate adult male villagers. The text is, in other words, a unique snapshot of the adult male élite of Aphrodito in 547/548. After the text of the petition fifty-one villagers sign their names in the following order:[27]

Victor, priest of the major church of Aphrodito and presumably Dioscorus' cousin, in which case he was the Victor who accompanied his uncle and Dioscorus' father Apollos on a previous visit to Constantinople in A.D. 541 (see *P.Cair.Masp.* II 67126)

---

26 See on this text L.S.B. MacCoull, op. cit. (note 20 above) 21-22.

27 For family members of Dioscorus, see the family tree on p. 131. For an explanation of "collective taxpayer," see the note on line 1a in the commentary.

Promaos, son of Iohannes; Petrus; Anuphis; Psaïs; Callinicus; Victor; Eulogius; another Victor; and Abrahamius, nine priests of nine less important churches; only the last one, Abrahamius, is illiterate and has his lector Pheüs sign for him

Callinicus, son of Dioscorus' cousin Victor, who accompanied Dioscorus on a later visit to Constantinople in 551 (see *P.Cair.Masp.* I 67032); Apollos; Lucanus; and Phoebammon, presumably the Phoebammon of our text, all four landowners

Ieremias, son of Victor, a notary known from *P.Cair.Masp.* II 67133, who here signs also on behalf of Constantinus, son of Hermauos, the chief bronze-smith; Dorantinous, son of Iosephius, a wine-merchant; Iosephius, son of Apollos, the chief fuller; Phoebammon, son of Papnuthius, the chief carpenter; Horuonchis, son of Matheias, the chief basket-weaver; and Ieremias, son of Phibius, the chief boatwright, because all six of them are illiterate

Pilatus, another notary known from other documents,[28] who signs here also for three others, Promauos, son of Apollos; Iosephius, son of Iohannes, a landowner; and Macarius, son of Iosephius, the chief-[occupation lost], because all three are illiterate

Senuthes, the village chief (*protokometes*), Apollos' son and Dioscorus' brother, who accompanied Dioscorus on a later visit to Constantinople in 551 (see *P.Cair.Masp.* I 67032), where he represented Cyrus, son of his cousin Victor, who signs towards the end of the document

Apollos, a landowner

Apollos, son of Iosephius, the collector of money taxes, who subscribes for an illiterate in *P.Lond.* V 1702

Georgius, son of Psempnuthes, a deacon who is also a landowner

Isac, son of Musaeus, and Phoebammon, son of Psenthaesius, known from *P.Lond.* V 1844, two illiterate landowners; and Triadelphus, son of Constantinus, who signs on their behalf as well as on his own

Hermauos, an assistant tax collector

Aurelius Iacob, son of Phoebammon, a collective taxpayer

---

28 See J.M. Diethart & K.A. Worp, *Notarsunterschriften im byzantinischen Ägypten* (Vienna, 1986) 30-31, where texts ranging in date from 547 to 566 are listed. It should be noted that this work gives information about notarial subscriptions only and therefore does not include *P.Cair.Masp.* II 67283, which tells us more about Pilatus' social status than all the other texts taken together.

Isac, son of Iohannes, for whom Dioscorus' father Apollos once acted as middleman in 526 (see *P.Cair.Masp.* I 67102); Abraham, son of Anuphius, who is illiterate and has Enoch, son of Heracleius, sign for him (Enoch does so for a woman in *P.Cair.Masp.* I 67092 in 553); Phoebammon, son of Phibius, known as a witness from *P.Vat.Aphrod.* 7; Mathias, son of Iosephius, known as a witness from *P.Cair.Masp.* II 67127 of 544; and Amaïs, son of Abrahamius, who wrote *P.Cair.Masp.* II 67127 of 544, all five landowners

Flavius Dioscorus, son of Megas, a landowner, and Dioscorus' cousin[29]

Flavius Theotecnus, son of Psaius, a landowner and a former deputy official, who acts as a witness in *P.Lond.* V 1687 of 523 and *P.Cair.Masp.* II 67128 of 547 and who subscribes for illiterates in *P.Cair.Masp.* II 67127 of 544 and *P.Lond.* V 1693

Cyrus, son of Dioscorus' cousin Victor, and Abraham, son of Victor, a witness in *P.Cair.Masp.* II 67128 of 547, who subscribes for an illiterate in *P.Cair.Masp.* I 67001 of 514, both landowners

Iezeciel, son of Victor, the chief wine-merchant

Enoch, son of Hermauos, and Flavius C[rest of the name lost], both landowners

Flavius Bessurus

Chrystes and Callinicus, son of Hermauos, a witness in *P.Cair.Masp.* I 67110 of 565

Palos, priest and caretaker of yet another church, who is illiterate and has the monk Iohannes sign on his behalf

Iohannes, son of Cornelius, a landowner who subscribes for an illiterate in *P.Lond.* V 1687 of 523

The order of the signatures is by no means accidental. First comes a group of clergymen, who are given pride of place because of their religious and social prestige. They are headed by the priest of the most important church in Aphrodito, who happens to be Dioscorus' own cousin (if our identification is correct). Next comes a group of four landowners, presumably the wealthier and more prestigious ones, followed by two notaries. These notaries also represent a number of illiterates, most of whom are craftsmen. Only then the village chief, Dioscorus' brother Senuthes, follows. The rest of the signatures follow in more or less random order. It is not clear what procedure was followed in appending the signatures to the petition. Dioscorus may have gone from

---

29 The editor identifies the hand with that of Dioscorus himself. See our note on line 3 in the commentary.

one end of Aphrodito to the other to solicit the individual signatures. In that case Dioscorus first devised an order for the signatures on the basis of his own perception of status and prestige in Aphrodito, but it is difficult to see where the initiative for the petition came from in the first place and why the notaries also sign for other people.

It is therefore more likely that there was a general meeting of the adult male inhabitants of Aphrodito to discuss the petition, followed by a signing ceremony. On that occasion the social hierarchy of Aphrodito was dramatically confirmed by the order observed in the act of appending the signatures. The priest Victor would have come forward first, audibly or implicitly invited to do so by those present at the meeting. After his colleagues signed the more important landowners followed. Only then the representatives of the professional crafts got their turn, but because they were illiterate, they had to be represented by two notaries. The order of the signatures therefore suggests that the ideological constructs of hierarchy and power were fully entrenched in the society of late antique Aphrodito. The inhabitants had a clear idea of their own position, and in case they ever forgot, social dramas like the signing ceremony could refresh their memory.

Among fifty-one signatories there are fourteen individuals who describe themselves as illiterates. This may simply mean that they did not know how to write Greek, the language of choice used for the petition including the signatures. The empress Theodora was supposed to read the petition and could not be expected to read Coptic. Some of the individual signatories may have been fluent in Coptic,[30] Egyptian written in Greek letters with the addition of a few ancient Egyptian characters to express sounds that did not have equivalents in the Greek alphabet. The distribution of literacy and illiteracy over the various groups represented among the signatories is markedly uneven. Only two out of twelve clergymen and four out of twenty-two landowners are illiterate. But only one out of eight representatives of the professional crafts is literate. Literacy did not by itself confer social status high enough to cause a person's inclusion as a signatory in the list. Not all the signatories are literate and only three out of six of those who sign for the illiterates also sign for themselves.[31]

30 Cf. J.G. Keenan, "On Languages and Literacy in Byzantine Aphrodito," *Proc. XVIII Int. Congr. Papyr.*, Vol. 2 (Athens, 1988): 161-67.

31 On literacy in late antique Egypt in general, see E. Wipszycka, "Le degré d'alphabétisation en Égypte byzantine," *RÉAug* 30 (1984): 279-96. She notes an increase in literacy over the earlier Roman period, but as usual this is based more

By appending their signatures to the petition addressed to the empress the adult male élite of Aphrodito contrived to defend their common interests against the authorities in Antaeopolis. Rarely do modern scholars of late antiquity enjoy such a display of an ancient civic virtue. The petition was the medium of choice to express the will of the community. Particularly the individual signatures provide us with a key to a better understanding of the social stratification of late antique Aphrodito, as we have seen, and it also shows the basis on which the higher social strata exercised their political power in the village. After all, the petition is not signed by the entire population of Aphrodito, but by individuals with clout in the community. The majority of them are landowners (22 out of 51) and representatives of the local churches (12 out of 51). Because these ecclesiastical institutions also owned a considerable amount of land, we might as well regard these clergymen as an additional group of landowners. This underscores the fact that the economy of Aphrodito was rooted in agriculture and that power derived from landownership. Some professions and trades are represented in the petition as well, but tenants and shepherds have been excluded. People in these categories were regarded as transient and unstable elements in society,[32] who had no property of their own. Although two wine-merchants are mentioned, no other trades related to the food industry in Aphrodito are represented. It seems that only the most respectable crafts, which needed special skills and brought higher profits, are included.

The petition is a "show of power" and the inclusion or exclusion of certain classes and social groups is indicative of the perception of power in late antique society. Most tellingly, no women are mentioned in the list. Aphrodito was a male-dominated society. Most members of the adult male élite are literate in Greek and know how to make use of writing and written documents as a means of exercising their political and economic power.

In conclusion, we think that the petition to the empress also acts as a link between the past and the present, because it helps us to relate our experience as citizens of our own communities with that of Egyptian villagers fifteen centuries ago. In modern times petitions with signatures are still employed to bring to the attention of governments general or

---

on impressions than on solid statistical evidence. Traditionally the opposite has been argued.

32 See J.G. Keenan, "Village Shepherds and Social Tension in Byzantine Egypt," *YCS* 28 (1985): 245-59.

specific issues, especially when public opinion is in opposition to the decisions of the central or local authorities.

No statistical figures exist for the size of the population of Aphrodito. We can do no more than suggest a total population of several thousands at any given moment in the sixth century A.D. We do know several thousand inhabitants of late antique Aphrodito at least by name.[33] Most of them are adult males, as one would expect in a male-dominated society. The literate adult males are most visible in our documentation, because these were often asked to append their signatures as witnesses to all kinds of private documents. Custom prescribed the presence of at least three witnesses to such documents. The number of signatories could be much larger. The document we publish also closes with the signatures of witnesses, but because the text is damaged at the bottom, we cannot decide whether the fifth witness was followed by one or two more witnesses. Even with the overrepresentation of adult males, and especially of the literate among them, a more or less convincing picture of the professional population of late antique Aphrodito emerges.[34] Many trades and crafts are represented, such as basket-weavers, bronze-smiths, carpenters, cooks, shepherds, vetch-sellers, wine-merchants, etc. Also the professions related to the river trade are well represented, because the town was located on a branch of the Nile. The range of professions is wider and more diversified than one would perhaps expect in a village with a strictly agricultural base. We do not want to create the false impression that Aphrodito's economy was not predominantly agricultural. The craftsmen cannot overshadow the landowners, middlemen, and tenants combined, but their impact on the social structure should not be dismissed as insignificant. The diversity of Aphrodito's professional population can be paralleled by the early Roman evidence from the larger towns in the Arsinoite nome, such as Karanis and Philadelphia.

In Aphrodito many men and women owned land in large and small parcels. The texts describe them all as landowners without further indication of their everyday profession. It is likely that those with small holdings farmed their land themselves, while those with substantial holdings leased at least some of their land to tenants. Still others subleased to tenants land they did not own themselves. These middlemen or entrepreneurs are well represented in our documentation from late an-

---

33 See the prosopography of V.A. Girgis, *Prosopografia e Afroditopolis* (Berlin, 1938), which lists almost 2,000 individuals from papyri published up to 1938.

34 See L.S.B. MacCoull, "Notes on the Social Structure of Late Antique Aphrodito," *BSAC* 26 (1984): 65-77.

tique Aphrodito.[35] They own capital goods such as animals and other agricultural equipment, and they have no difficulty in finding the cash to buy seed or pay laborers for the maintenance of local irrigation systems and the performance of other agricultural tasks their tenants would or could not perform themselves. Apollos, the father of Dioscorus and one of the key figures in our text, was such a middleman, and he may well have made his fortune by leasing land from larger landowners from nearby Antaeopolis or other nome capitals, who owned land around Aphrodito, or from the monasteries and churches of the region, and subleasing it to tenants. His long-time position in the town as its "chief" or *protokometes* shows that he ranked among the richest inhabitants of his hometown.

All this contrasts with what we know about the Oxyrhynchite nome in late antiquity, where the middlemen seem almost to have disappeared from the scene. However, this seems to be no more than a streak in the admittedly abundant Oxyrhynchite documentation that overwhelmingly relates to a particular family of absentee landowners, the Flavii Apiones. The papers of that family have always been regarded as sufficient documentary evidence for the traditional notion that the Roman empire in late antiquity was merely a collection of large estates. But the evidence for middlemen at the local level in Aphrodito[36] as well as the evidence for the distribution of landed wealth from the Hermopolite nome in the fourth century A.D. [37] seems to bring out a significantly different and more diverse picture of the society and economy of late antique Egypt. The landed wealth of the medium and small landowners combined exceeded that of the really big landowners, mainly resident in the nome capitals. The former groups and the entrepreneurs among them played an important role in the agricultural economy of Egypt in late antiquity. The well-to-do inhabitants of Aphrodito, which is once described as a town consisting of small landowners (see *P.Lond.* V 1674, 95-96), were the ones who, like Apollos, were most successful in exploiting the land of absentee landowners in

---

35 See J.G. Keenan, "Aurelius Phoibammon, Son of Triadelphus: A Byzantine Egyptian Land Entrepreneur," *BASP* 17 (1980): 145-54. Examples are Dioscorus himself, his father Apollos, his uncle Besarion and his cousin's husband Phoebammon.

36 See J.G. Keenan, "Notes on Absentee Landlordism at Aphrodito," *BASP* 22 (1985): 137-69.

37 See A.K. Bowman, "Landholding in the Hermopolite Nome in the Fourth Century," *JRS* 75 (1985): 137-63.

addition to the land they owned themselves. For all we know, landownership and its exploitation may have been as varied in late antique Egypt as it had been in early Roman Egypt. It may be significant that a major figure in the Oxyrhynchite evidence relating to the exploitation of land owned by the Flavii Apiones, the so-called *colonus adscripticius* (usually explained as "serfs bound to the soil"), has not yet been attested in the documentation from the rest of Egypt.[38] And yet the serf-like figure of the *colonus adscripticius* has always been an important prop for the traditional notion of late antique society as a form of nascent "feudalism." We will not pursue here the revisionist thesis that is gaining more ground in recent literature on this topic.[39]

In assessing the importance of the various types of landownership in late antique Egypt one should also take the land owned by churches and monasteries into account. These new institutions of Christian Egypt had quite an impact on the ownership of land in Aphrodito. Almost a third of all land in the cadastre of Aphrodito, which was drawn up just before the accession of Justinian to the throne, belonged to seven monasteries. The same cadastre also indicates how much land belonged to Aphrodito as a whole: almost 6,000 arouras (4,125 acres, an aroura being roughly three quarters of an acre), an amount not unlike that known for other larger towns in earlier Roman Egypt.[40] Almost all of the land at Aphrodito was arable, but a significant proportion of it, almost 11.5 percent, was occupied by gardens and vineyards.[41]

It has been suggested with some degree of justification that Aphrodito could become the Montaillou of late antiquity.[42] If this suggestion has a ring of truth to it, it is not simply because the papyri pro-

---

38 See the summary in I.F. Fikhman, "De nouveau sur le colonat du Bas Empire," *Miscellanea papyrologica in occasione del bicentenario dell'edizione della Charta Borgiana,* Vol. 1 (Florence, 1990): 159-79.

39 For references, see, e.g., T. Gagos & P. van Minnen, "Documenting the Rural Economy of Byzantine Egypt: Three Papyri from Alabastrine," *JRA* 5 (1992): 186-202.

40 The evidence can be traced with the help of D.W. Rathbone, "Villages, Land and Population in Graeco-Roman Egypt," *PCPhS* 36 (1990): 103-42.

41 See *P.Cair.Masp.* I 67057 III with the comments in J. Gascou & L.S.B. MacCoull, "Le cadastre d'Aphroditô," *T&M* 10 (1987): 118.

42 See J.G. Keenan, "The Aphrodito Papyri and Village Life in Byzantine Egypt," *BSAC* 26 (1984): 56, referring to the work of the French historian É. Le Roy Ladurie on late medieval Languedoc.

vide evidence for a substantial reconstruction of the social and economic history of the village or because the kind of evidence we have provides a good story teller with the opportunity to fashion an intelligent recreation of village life, long stilled by the lapse of time. It is also because of the nature of the evidence, which happens to come from the archive of a single person, Dioscorus, who transmits the silenced voices of his fellow villagers as well as his own. Such an archive provides the best ancient parallel to the data base for late medieval Montaillou. Texts can be one-sided in their information, since they were written by one person. They may also be records of ordinary activities in a village, as is the case with many of Dioscorus' business papers, or records of one extraordinary type of activity, as is the case with the inquisition reports from Montaillou and Dioscorus' poems. But they are a bridge between our society and that of the distant past, no matter whether it is late antique Egypt or late medieval Languedoc.

4. *Between the law and the lyre: the personal papers of Dioscorus*

Your Greek is always elegant and musical.
But we want all your craftsmanship now.
Our sorrow and our love move into a foreign language.
Pour your Egyptian feeling into the Greek you use.

Raphael, your verses, you know, should be written
so they contain something of our life within them,
so the rhythm, so every phrase clearly shows
that an Alexandrian is writing about an Alexandrian.

C.P. Cavafy, *Collected Poems* (revised ed., Princeton, 1992) 71.

We know sixth-century Aphrodito mainly through one channel of information: the papers of Dioscorus. A significant monograph devoted to Dioscorus is now available.[43] Its focus is on his poems and their social and cultural context rather than on his ordinary papers. Opportunities to reconstruct Dioscorus' world through these papers still exist, and we will attempt to reconstruct one aspect of it in sections 9-10. Here we provide some basic background information on Dioscorus to aid the study of the

43 L.S.B. MacCoull, op. cit. (note 20 above). See the review by E. Wipszycka, *Biblioteca Orientalis* 48 (1991): 529-36.

text we publish. The text itself predates the active phase of Dioscorus' career by several years. Dioscorus' oldest datable piece of work is from A.D. 543, but his first official text, the petition we discussed at length in the previous section, dates from 547/548. Several members of Dioscorus' family play an important role in our text. The family tree (see p. 131) will help to clarify relationships between the descendants of Psimanobet, great-grandfather of Dioscorus the notary, poet, lawyer, administrator, property owner, and man of affairs.

In our text Dioscorus' father Apollos acts as the representative of Dioscorus' cousin Anastasia and her husband Phoebammon. Apollos is known to us as early as A.D. 514 (see *P.Flor.* III 280) as a creditor and village chief (*protokometes*). He founded a monastery in 538, probably not long after the present text was written, visited Constantinople in 541 (see *P.Cair.Masp.* II 67126) and died in the fiscal year 546/547.[44] It seems as if Dioscorus had to wait until his father's death to become independently active in the affairs of his community.

Dioscorus himself was born about six years after his father's earliest appearance in our sources, around A.D. 520, and he is last attested in 585. Dioscorus was given his grandfather's name in accordance with the widespread practice of papponymy. His father's grandfather had an Egyptian name, Psimanobet, "the son of the gooseherd." This by no means implies that he was of humble origin, but at least suggests that the family's roots were not in the traditional Greek élite of Egypt. As was common for children of well-to-do families, Dioscorus had a good education, presumably in the Greek classics and Roman law.[45] There is no evidence that he read much Coptic literature, such as the martyrologies that became so popular later, or that he found much inspiration in the theological writings in Coptic by Shenute and others. Still, he was very much rooted in both Greek and Egyptian culture as is clear from his fluency in writing both Coptic and Greek. As a notary he wrote Coptic as well as Greek documents on request. His training as a notary was therefore bilingual, and that training involved even more *belles lettres* than Roman law. In a Greek-Coptic glossary Dioscorus collected obscure poetic Greek words and tried to give simple Coptic equivalents for each. As far as we can tell from the Greek documents he wrote, Dioscorus was

---

44 On Apollos see especially J.G. Keenan, "Aurelius Apollos and the Aphrodite Village Élite," *Atti XVII congr. intern. papir.*, Vol. 3 (Naples, 1984): 957-63. To the documents discussed there, add *P.Vat.Aphrod.* 7 where Apollos acts as a witness.

45 See L.S.B. MacCoull, op. cit. (note 20 above) 8-9.

a master of the late antique prose style.[46] His texts are wordy, keen on making the structure of the argument stand out and ever ready to improvise aptly the same old purple patches. Dioscorus owned a few works of Greek literature: Homer (*P.Cair.Masp.* II 67172-74, which constitute one manuscript), some comedies of Menander (see also section 9) and a biography of the Attic orator Isocrates (*P.Cair.Masp.* II 67175). He presumably did not personally own any other literature–it would not have escaped the attention of those who excavated or plundered his house in modern times. It is remarkable that in his poems Dioscorus himself explicitly refers only to the three authors mentioned. The codex containing the comedies of Menander also contains a comedy by Eupolis (fr. 99 Kassel-Austin), identified as such in modern times on the basis of a quotation. Dioscorus may not have been aware of this at all, and he presumably regarded it as another comedy by Menander.

Dioscorus also attempted to write Greek poems in hexameters and iambic trimeters, without much success, although he himself thought otherwise. When praising an official called Romanus in iambics and hexameters, Dioscorus presents his hexameter poem as follows:[47] "You deserve the best: here you are, Sir" (κάλλιϲτά ϲοι πρέπει· δέχου, ὦ δέϲποτα). This and the other poems have met with severe criticism and condemnation by earlier scholars and with little appreciation among modern readers. It has become part of the traditional discourse in dealing with Dioscorus' poems to voice this lack of appreciation.

More recent studies have adopted a revisionist thesis and have succeeded in providing a context for appreciating this poetry.[48] To be sure, most of these poems are not great works of literature, especially when compared with their illustrious classical models. However, these poems are invaluable as "contemporary witnesses" (*Zeitdokumente*) for the social history of literature. They give us a unique insight into the intense literary climate of Upper Egypt in the sixth century. Dioscorus spent several years from A.D. 566 to 573 in the capital of the Lower Thebais, Antinoopolis, where he had ample opportunity to get acquainted with the great literature of his time. Most of it was after all

---

46 See the discussion in L.S.B. MacCoull, op. cit. (note 20 above) 16-36.

47 See P. van Minnen, "Isocrates and Menander in Late Antique Perspective," *GRBS* 30 (1992): 90.

48 See L.S.B. MacCoull, op. cit. (note 20 above) and, more recently, P. van Minnen, op. cit. (note 47 above): 87-98, and C.A. Kuehn, "A New Papyrus of a Dioscorian Poem and Marriage Contract," *ZPE* 97 (1993): 103-15.

written in the Thebais or by poets originating in that province.[49] Dioscorus' literary home is therefore not just an Egyptian village like Aphrodito. His poetry consists of laudatory poems for local officials and of mythological extravaganzas centered on the local traditions. His themes always seem to articulate the concerns of the local élite and of the intellectuals of this era: power, patronage, and the church. From these themes we can sense his awareness of the dynamic function of poetry in sixth-century society. The poems comment in their own way on political, social, and religious developments and institutions in provincial Egypt. Only if we approach Dioscorus from this point of view can we learn to appreciate his contributions to Greek poetry, and we can appreciate even better those of his more succesful contemporaries such as Nonnus, who wrote two long epic poems, one on a strictly pagan theme (the *Dionysiaca*), and one on a Christian theme (the paraphrase of the Gospel of John). In Dioscorus' poems and also in some of the legal documents these two themes are often deftly interwoven, especially in the laudatory poems. In other poems he stays close to the classical, pagan models.[50]

Before moving to Antinoopolis and while his father was still alive and running his monastery, Dioscorus receives once (*P.Cair.Masp.* I 67064) the flattering epithet *scholastikos*: not just a notary, but an official trained in the legal doctrine of his age and associated with the legal administration. By moving to Antinoopolis, the legal and administrative center of the Lower Thebais, Dioscorus sought to attain this social status, something he could not achieve in Aphrodito, where he had already reached the topmost rank with his position as notary and landowner. In Antinoopolis he must have soon reached the limit of his own abilities.

The function of men like Dioscorus changed considerably in the course of his lifetime. In the thirties of the sixth century the great codification of the traditions of Roman law was put into final shape under the inspiration of the emperor Justinian. After that, knowledge of and versatility in applying this large body of rules became a sine qua non

49 A. Cameron, "Wandering Poets: A Literary Movement in Byzantine Egypt," *Historia* 14 (1965): 470-509, and G.W. Bowersock, *Hellenism in Late Antiquity* (Ann Arbor, 1990) 55-69, especially 63. For a corpus of fragments of such poetry, see E. Heitsch, *Die griechischen Dichterfragmente der römischen Kaiserzeit*, Vol. 1 (Göttingen, 1961).

50 See G.W. Bowersock, op. cit. (note 49 above) 68-69.

for a public career. Dioscorus may have been one of the first students to learn to apply these rules, if his legal training started at age 14 or thereabouts. Through the legal documents, testaments, sales, petitions, settlements, etc., he composed over the course of years we can study him as a writer of legal prose. Documents in late antiquity tended to be very long and sometimes longwinded, as we shall see in section 8. Thus, the scribe of our document seems aware of his own prolixity (see especially lines 75-76). Most documents from the hand of Dioscorus and his contemporaries contain several standard formulas. It is, however, the presentation of the individual case, unique in every instance, that provided Dioscorus with the best opportunity to show his talent as a prose writer.

Dioscorus also collected and copied documents written by others. Some of them undoubtedly interested him because of their literary merits, such as the petition of Horapollon, the author of a treatise on ancient Egyptian hieroglyphics (see *P.Cair.Masp.* III 27295 I). But presumably Dioscorus kept the majority of these documents as models in case he needed to deal with an affair that paralleled the one treated by a colleague. In this way Dioscorus also preserved the document that we publish here. It was written on behalf of his cousin, Anastasia also called Tecrompia, and her husband Phoebammon, but in their absence it was Dioscorus' father, Apollos, who received the document and took it back home to Aphrodito, where it eventually entered Dioscorus' archive after his father's death. By the time the document was written Dioscorus was a teenager just about to embark upon the study of Roman law, possibly in Alexandria. After his father died Dioscorus automatically assumed a position as a leading man in his community, along with his brothers and his cousins. Dioscorus and his brother Senuthes both succeeded their father Apollos as village chief (*protokometes*) sometime after the latter established a monastery in Aphrodito in A.D. 538, following the model of the Bawit monastery, which was situated halfway between Aphrodito and Antinoopolis and was founded by Apollos' great model, his namesake Apa Apollos, more than a century earlier. Senuthes is one of the witnesses in our text. He probably was a little older than his brother Dioscorus. Their cousin Anastasia undoubtedly was one of the leading women in her community, although we do not know her as well as her male relatives. She married one of the more enterprising men in sixth-century Aphrodito, Phoebammon, son of Triadelphus. Like Dioscorus' brother Senuthes Anastasia also has an Egyptian name–her other name Tecrompia means "the dove."

5. *Date of the settlement*

The exact date of our document can no longer be established, because the text is broken off at the top. This lost portion must have contained a reference to the day on which it was written, because there is a reference to "the present and abovementioned day" in lines 60-61. It is however very likely that the document was drawn up some time between A.D. 527, the date of the accession to the throne of Justinian–who is mentioned in the text–and 538, the year Apollos founded his own monastery and became known as the "most worshipful Apa Apollos." A likely date towards the end of this period is supported by the imperial oath in lines 77-79 of the text, the only parallel for which dates from 537, and it would not be too far from the truth to speculate that the document was in fact drawn up in 537, the year preceding the foundation of the monastery. This squares well with the fact that Apollos is still playing an active role in the secular matters with which our papyrus deals.[51]

6. *Content of the settlement*

The document we edit here is a prime example of a late antique notarial deed drawn up in Antinoopolis, the capital of Lower Thebais. The text records the settlement of a dispute over a piece of property and it refers to itself as a *dialytike homologia* (literally: an agreement [*homologia*] relating to a settlement [*dialysis*]). The document settles a dispute between Aurelius Nicantinous on the one hand and Aurelius Phoebammon and his wife Aurelia Anastasia, also called Tecrompia, on the other hand. Anastasia[52] is a cousin of Dioscorus, as we have seen at the end of section

51 For additional information on the date, see also the note to line 4 of our commentary with further references to secondary literature, as well as the note to lines 77-79.

52 From now on we omit the names Aurelius or Aurelia in referring to the principal characters involved in the dispute. In this we follow the practice of the document itself. The presence or absence of Aurelius or Aurelia is not without

4. Dioscorus' father Apollos, *protokometes* or village chief of Aphrodito at the time the document was drawn up, represents his niece Anastasia and her husband Phoebammon in Antinoopolis.

The dispute concerns a piece of land, presumably a vineyard because the text refers to it several times as a *ktema*.[53] Some time before the present dispute arose the *ktema* was owned by the parents of Nicantinous, who used it to secure a loan from the parents of Iosephius. Iosephius' parents had the contract of loan drawn up with their son as lender, no doubt to give the lad some future financial security. This older generation has apparently died and they are not mentioned as parties to the dispute. As often happens, the next generation has inherited not only the property but also the debts. So, Iosephius inherited the loan contract from his parents, but while Nicantinous inherited the liability of his parents' debt, his nieces and nephew seem to have inherited the property itself. Although selling property under lien was illegal according to Greco-Roman law,[54] unless the creditors gave their consent,[55] Nicantinous' young kinsmen have done just that: they sold the estate to Phoebammon and Anastasia. Iosephius may have notified Phoebammon and Anastasia of the lien he held over the property they purchased. In any case, the couple begins to contemplate taking action against Nicantinous and his family, and their representative, Apollos, finds himself in Antinoopolis with Nicantinous. After a long period of deliberations, with the advice of mediators, both parties reach an agreement, whereby Nicantinous pays off the debt he inherited from his parents, thus cancelling Iosephius' lien

---

significance. As a rule the presence of Aurelius or Aurelia denotes an ordinary citizen of the later Roman empire, its absence a member of the clergy. Contrast the note on line 1a in the commentary with those on lines 106 and 113.

53 See the commentary on line 12.

54 See especially the stipulations in a document that concerns a loan secured by property, *P.Warr.* 10, 23-26 (A.D. 591/592), where we read: "and we will not be allowed to take the one and a half *aroura* [roughly an acre of land] away from the security and sell it or use it as security for another loan or otherwise, until we pay this loan back in full" (καὶ μ̣[ὴ ἐξέϲτω ἡμῖν τὴν] μίαν ἥμιϲυ ἄρουραν ἀποϲπᾶν τῆϲ ὑ̣[ποθήκηϲ ἄχριϲ] ἀποδόϲεωϲ καὶ ϲυμπληρώϲεωϲ τ[οῦ αὐτοῦ χρέουϲ καὶ] μὴ πωλεῖν, μὴ ὑποθέϲθαι, μηδὲ ἄλλ[ωϲ πωϲ οἰκονομεῖν]); similar stipulations are found in *PSI* XIII 1340, 14-16 (420); and *SB* I 5285, 36-42 (607).

55 See, e.g., *P.Berl.Frisk* 5 of A.D. 510, where the creditor, a woman, allows her debtor, another woman, to use a piece of property under lien as security for a loan from her.

on the property, and ratifies the previous sale of the property. In return, the new owners are to pay Nicantinous an indemnity in cash (seven solidi minus two carats each) and in kind (twenty artabas of wheat). Phoebammon and Anastasia were forced to accept this term of the settlement, perhaps because they had paid less than the market value when they purchased the property under lien. It is also possible that they were able to get a bargain from the relatives of Nicantinous, because they were still under age. Such a situation is documented by **#32.**[56]

Nicantinous is involved on two counts: he is the heir of his parents' debt and he more or less represents his nephew and nieces who sold the property while it was still under lien. Presumably neither the buyers of the property, Phoebammon and Anastasia, nor the sellers, the nephew and nieces of Nicantinous, are present in Antinoopolis to deal with the matter themselves. In a way Nicantinous represents his nephew and nieces to help clean up the mess they perhaps unwittingly helped to create. It is also possible that they are under age and that Nicantinous acts on their behalf as their guardian, but that is by no means a necessary assumption. The dispute was settled in Antinoopolis, because as the capital of the Thebais it attracted all important legal transactions involving the courts. The settlement is even drawn up in the very building, the civil courthouse (line 9), where the matter would have been decided if it had been taken to court. Phoebammon and Anastasia may well have considered taking the matter to court, and this is perhaps implied in the phrase: "before a lawsuit and before cognition trials took place" (line 20). But it seems that they changed their minds and both parties agreed to avoid the complicated, time-consuming, and costly court procedures (see also section 10). Thus, they agree to make use of the only other alternative available: to settle their dispute "out of court" through mediation (see also section 9). The mediators are adult males described as "good friends," mostly from Aphrodito, who are visiting Antinoopolis for some unstated purpose.

Both the new owners and Nicantinous are in a somewhat awkward position. If Nicantinous were not willing to pay his parents' debt to Iosephius, then the property, which was used as security for the original loan, would continue to be under Iosephius' lien. Therefore, Iosephius could claim the property if Phoebammon and Anastasia were unable or unwilling to come up with the money. Nicantinous, on the other hand, is held accountable for the illegal sale of his parents' property. From a legal

---

56 Numbers in bold type throughout this monograph refer to our list on pp. 121-7.

standpoint Nicantinous is indeed in a precarious position, and that is probably why he issues the agreement of settlement and not Phoebammon and Anastasia or both parties together. The document is written in the form of an agreement in the first person singular and Nicantinous is the subject. However, it is also possible that Phoebammon and Anastasia drew up an agreement of settlement of their own in favor of Nicantinous, which has not survived, because it did not form part of the papers of Phoebammon, but of those of Nicantinous. The papers of Phoebammon are preserved within their kinsman Dioscorus' archive.[57] Nicantinous' papers have perished. It is clear that the document was transferred to Aphrodito after it was drawn up, because it was found there.

7. *Outline of the settlement*

Because of the length of the text we present an outline of it here. This clarifies both the flow of the argument and the construction of the Greek. The dating formula at the beginning is lost. Note that this outline is also used in the the paragraph division of the reading text and the facing English translation as well as in the commentary.

Date (lost)

Address (1a-5)

Agreement proper (5-98)

- (i) General statement by Nicantinous (5-6)
- (ii) Background of the case (6-28)
  - (a) Facts leading up to the present case (6-17)
  - (b) Mediation leading up to the present agreement (17-28)
- (iii) Terms and conditions (28-81)

  Putting the agreement down in writing means that it now becomes formal and definitive. The terms and conditions are expressed through a series of infinitives dependent on "I acknowledge" (28-34: ὁμολογῶ):

  - (a) receipt of payment towards the redemption of the property under lien to the new owners, Phoebammon and Anastasia, preceded by a brief recapitulation of the background: "I acknowledge that I have received

57 See the note on lines 1-2 in the commentary.

and have been paid by you" (34-40: ὁμολογῶ . . . εἰληφέναι μὲν καὶ πεπληρῶcθαι)

(b) renunciation of claims on the part of the original owner, Nicantinous; he and his heirs and successors will not claim the disputed property: "(I acknowledge) that I have or will have no claim against you" (40-51: [ὁμολογῶ] . . . μηδένα λόγον ἔχειν ἢ ἕξειν πρὸc ὑμᾶc . . .)

(c) confirmation of ownership of the new owners, Phoebammon and Anastasia, on the property in return for the payment received: "(I acknowledge) that you have the possession and the ownership" (51-57: [ὁμολογῶ] . . . ἔχειν ὑμᾶc . . . τὴν νομὴν καὶ τὴν δεcποτείαν . . .)

(d) settlement proper: the original owner, Nicantinous, will refrain from legal action against the new owners, Phoebammon and Anastasia, and their heirs and successors; reiteration of the receipt of the payment: "(I acknowledge) that I am reconciled and settled with you (57), and that no legal action is left for me against you (58), and that I am not able to proceed against you (62), but that any legal action whatsoever against you has become extinct for me (67)" (57-76: [ὁμολογῶ] . . . ἀπηλλάχθαι καὶ διαλελύcθαι πρὸc ὑμᾶc (57), . . . καὶ μηδεμίαν μοι . . . cῴζεcθαι . . . ἀγωγήν (58), . . . καὶ μὴ δύναcθαί με . . . ἐγκαλεῖν ὑμῖν . . . (62), . . . ἀλλὰ καὶ ἐcβέcθαι μοι καθ' ὑμῶν . . . οἱανδήποτε ἀγωγήν . . . (67))

(iv) Oath sworn in the name of the emperor that the original owner, Nicantinous, will comply with the terms and conditions of the settlement (76-81)

(v) Penalty clause for breaking the terms and the conditions of the agreement (82-96)

(vi) Clause validating the agreement (96-98)

Signatures and subscription (98-116)

8. *Notarial practices in late antique Egypt*

The present document is a prime example of a late antique notarial deed, similar to many that have been drawn up by Dioscorus. As has been rightly argued,[58] "[a] legal document as it came from Dioscorus's pen was far from a dull, flat-footed, matter-of-fact record of a transaction. But it was also not simply a verbose exercise in the sound of one's own voice . . . Even more so than a poem, a legal document was a mirror of his world, inasmuch as it was a working reality that actually effected something." Our document was not drawn up by Dioscorus, but the deftness of the scribe of our text is not far from that of Dioscorus. The bare outline given above hardly brings out the artistic abilities of our notary, but it does reflect something of the complexity of the case, and the dexterity with which the case has been handled and put in writing. It is noteworthy that the present document is superseded in length by only a few other contemporary documents of the same type, such as **#20** in our list on pp. 121-7. No section is redundant in the document, not a word is wasted. As it appears from our detailed discussion in the commentary, our notary is familiar with current legislation, knows how to handle the various formulas and even has some knowledge of technical terms in Latin, which once infiltrate his text (see "rescript" in line 65). In general the text is highly formulaic, as is the case with almost all similar documents, but these formulas are by no means the empty shells that they are often taken for by editors of late antique papyri and even sometimes by legal historians of the age.[59] In our commentary we have tried to establish the meaning of these formulas in the context of the present settlement, as well as within the more general social context and the legal set-up of late antique Egypt. Moreover, the text is drawn up according to an established pattern that is also detectable in the other settlement agreements of similar date. All of them contain the same ingredients, such as the introduction of the disputing parties, the narration of the background and the object of the dispute as well as of the circumstances that led up to the settlement, and an elaborate section on the various terms and conditions under which the parties come to terms. In format they all resemble the outline given above for our document. We have collected these in the list on pp. 121-7. We have only collected the Greek examples, because the Coptic settlements largely postdate the Arab conquest.

The pattern common to all private settlements of late antiquity deserves an explanation. The similarities in linguistic, stylistic, and the-

58 L.S.B. MacCoull, op. cit. (note 20 above) 17.

59 See the note on line 9 in the commentary. See also our discussion in section 10 of a thesis advanced by A.A. Schiller and built on the assumption that some of the formulas bear no relation to late antique reality at all.

matic respects are not accidental, but owe their existence to two factors. First, the training of the notaries[60] who were primarily responsible for the production of these settlements was the same. As we have seen in the case of Dioscorus in section 4, it combined the study of the Greek classics with the study of current legislation and its application to everyday situations, not only in Egypt, but everywhere else in the Mediterranean world as well. Roman law, enacted either from the Old or from the New Rome, had gradually replaced local systems of law by successive attempts of late Roman emperors to codify the existing body of legal traditions, culminating in Justinian's legislative work in the thirties of the sixth century A.D. The evidence for Egypt is exceptionally rich and diversified, both geographically and thematically, and no parallel evidence survives for the rest of the Roman empire. If it did, it would have undoubtedly shown the same pattern.[61] Second, the notaries who were responsible for drawing up the settlements often imitated their predecessors, their colleagues or themselves because of the subject matter of the cases they treated, which were often very similar. Imitation was a form of reference to previous cases or, as one would call it today, to "precedents."

We also have drafts with many corrections, which allow us to follow the notary at work as he is trying to establish the final version of a document. An instructive example of a draft is **#36**, where the names of the parties and some of the particulars have not been incorporated into the text.[62] Undoubtedly, the document in its final stage would have contained the particulars in all their details. It is also possible that a document served merely as an exemplar, a model to be followed in similar cases and containing all the necessary ingredients and formulas required in similar circumstances. Individual names of parties could be omitted so that the document could be filled out for a similar case, as is seen in the modern legal practice of "boilerplate" documents. Such texts are **#37** and **#17**. Interestingly enough, **#16** is a wooden tablet with a school exercise in drawing up a *dialysis.*

The notaries had a pivotal role in the legal system of late antiquity. This system did not consist of legal norms and rules different from those prevailing in the early Roman empire, but radically changed the

---

60 Some work of late antique notaries can be traced with the help of the lists provided in J.M. Diethart & K.A. Worp, op.cit. (note 28 above).

61 See H.J. Wolff, "Der byzantinische Urkundenstil Ägyptens im Lichte der Funde von Nessana und Dura," *RIDA* III 8 (1961): 115-54.

62 See the thorough discussion in E. von Druffel, op. cit. (note 2 above) 10-25.

application of these norms and rules. More than ever before knowledge of the precise wording of the law was a preliminary to its correct application in each individual case. From the thirties of the sixth century onwards a large body of legal texts, which had existed for centuries, was given force of law and soon also circulated in a Greek translation. Concurrently the importance of the officials in charge of the law courts declined and the notaries became gradually more involved in deciding whether a case was worth going to court for. With the law in hand notaries could solve most legal problems effectively, presumably at lower costs than the law courts. This, as we shall see in section 10, was one of the main reasons for the burgeoning of private settlements, where notaries are the key figures, and the decline of lawsuits in regular civil courts.

Thus, even though notaries can hardly be conceived of as the prime movers in the development of law in late antiquity, their role could not be illustrated better than by reference to the career of Dioscorus. It is by no means a coincidence that we know the vicissitudes of many families in Aphrodito mainly through his papers.

9. *Mediation in its sociocultural context*

The settlement recorded in our text was reached through mediation (lines 20-22). Before we discuss this particular type of private settlement, we must give an overview of the various forms of dispute processing attested in our documentation. We have tried to classify the other settlements as best we could in the list on pp. 121-7. The evidence shows that disputants in late antique Egypt could resort to four slightly different methods of ending their disputes privately. (1) They could voluntarily get together and agree to end their conflict of interests without the intervention of a third party. They could then make the terms of their settlement formal in a notarial deed. This method is called *negotiation*, and from the list on pp. 121-7 it appears that this was a very common method. (2) One or more outsiders without any official capacity could be called upon to help the disputants to come to terms; this is called *mediation* or *conciliation*, and from the list it appears that this was also a very common method. The suggestions of the mediator(s) were advisory and not binding. (3) The disputants could choose an arbitrator and have him reach a binding decision after investigation; this is *arbitration* in the strict sense, and from the list it appears that this was not a very common method. (4) The disputing parties could go to a state official, but before a trial was initiated, he could suggest that they settle their dispute privately by choosing one of the other options. From the list of settlements it appears that officials were involved in a variety of ways. Our document can be classified as mediation or conciliation.

The list presents a sufficiently varied picture of the kinds of people involved in settling disputes as arbitrators or mediators. Sometimes mutual friends were asked to mediate, as in our text, where they are called "good friends." Sometimes one or more officials were invited to mediate. It was apparently important to choose mediators or arbitrators who had inside knowledge of the local situation and were respected in their community. Officials were called upon not so much in their official capacity, but as private individuals acceptable to both parties, presumably in cases where there were no mutual friends or the dispute transcended the confines of the local community. A curious case is presented by **#15**. A bishop and two priests are at odds with their deacon, Theophilus. He offers the bishop the choice between a lawsuit and a private settlement through mediation by two *scholastikoi*, legal experts. These clergymen apparently did not want to ask another man of the cloth to mediate between them. Maybe they could not find one acceptable to them all. Settlement through the so-called *audientia episcopalis* (a hearing before the bishop who acts as an arbitrator) may have been impossible, because one of the parties to the dispute happened to be a bishop himself.

What was the legal status of arbitration and mediation in late antiquity? Was the outcome of either in any way enforceable by law or did it solely depend on the goodwill of the parties to the dispute to abide by the terms of the settlement? We do not have to elaborate on these questions, because others have done that before.[63] We think that arbitration and mediation are forms of social discourse and should not be regarded as part of the legal process only. We do not believe that even the strictest form of dispute settlement, arbitration in the narrow sense, where the disputing parties have agreed to accept the outcome of the arbitration beforehand, was effective only because of the legal formulas included in the settlement document. Some of these did act as a deterrent against breaking the terms of the agreement, because of the fines and penalties to be paid to the other party or the government in case of

---

63 For a legal history approach, see K.-H. Ziegler, *Das private Schiedsgericht im antiken römischen Recht* (Munich, 1971). Ziegler discusses some late antique settlements on pp. 268-70 and provides a selective list on pp. 289-91.

breach of contract. But the most effective settlements were those where the mediators or arbitrators had carefully taken the ramifications of the case into account. They should not only consider the object of dispute and the facts of the case, but also the relationship between the parties. Often members of the same family were involved, and sometimes even the arbitrators and mediators were somehow related to the disputants, at least in the broad sense of being members of the same community. The mediators and arbitrators certainly did not want to be embarrassed in public by criticism of their work, voiced by supporters of either of the parties to the dispute. This fits in well with our legal-anthropological approach to settlements in general, as outlined in the next section. Even when government officials were called upon to act as mediators or arbitrators, the success of their action nevertheless depended on their ability to take the background of the disputants into account.

The distinction between the two categories of mediators and arbitrators is real.[64] Mediators discuss the matter with the disputing parties and suggest a solution. The parties then have to come up with the terms of the settlement, no doubt assisted in doing this by the mediators and the notary, who draws up the settlement document and can also give legal advice. Arbitrators also discuss the matter with the two parties to a dispute, but before the work of the arbitrators begins the parties have already agreed to accept the outcome of the arbitration by signing a so-called *compromissum* document. This step makes arbitration different from mediation in that it is binding. The party who does not accept the outcome of arbitration can be sued in court by the other party with the *compromissum* in hand. If one of the parties refuses to accept the outcome of mediation, however, the settlement process simply has to continue by other means, e.g., through a lawsuit, or arbitration, or negotiation, or mediation by other mediators.

In choosing between the options of mediation and arbitration the parties have to assess carefully the possible outcome of each method of settling their dispute with the help of outsiders. When the case is too complicated and has reached an impasse, as in #20, it is more likely that recourse is taken to arbitrators than to mediators; someone has to break the log jam or cut the Gordian knot. Where the dispute is over a simple problem or over a family matter, mediation may be preferable because the outcome of mediation can be more unobtrusively manipulated by the disputants than the outcome of arbitration. In our text mediation rather

---

64 As pointed out by A.A. Schiller, "The Courts Are No More," *Studi Edoardo Volterra*, Vol. 1 (Milan, 1969) 494.

than arbitration may have been chosen, because the matter involved a third party, Iosephius, whose interests also had to be taken into account, or because the stakes involved were not too high. We cannot really be certain about this, because the text does not tell us much about the negotiations preceding the mediation. The mediators' suggestion is adopted by the disputing parties, but it could have been altered substantially if they had wished to.

Apart from their social context the options of mediation and arbitration can also be studied within the cultural context of late antique Egypt. To do this we not only need to take documentary texts into account, but also literature and comparative material from other societies.[65] There is one instance of arbitration that plays a prominent role in a work of literature produced centuries earlier, but demonstrably read in late antique Egypt. A copy of it was actually found among the papers of Dioscorus. By this we mean the arbitration scene in Menander's *Epitrepontes* ("men submitting themselves to arbitration"), a play produced in Athens about the turn of the fourth and third centuries B.C. The codex from Dioscorus' archive, which contains several plays by Menander, was unearthed in 1905 along with many documentary texts.[66] Dioscorus' copy of the *Epitrepontes* is our only complete textual witness for the arbitration scene. Although we do not wish to suggest that there is a direct relation between any of the settlement cases from late antiquity that survive and the arbitration scene in the Attic comedy, there is a more subtle connection between those who actually produced these settlements and Menander's work. As a notary Dioscorus was intimately involved in documenting settlements and his copy of some of Menander's plays did not include the *Epitrepontes* by mere chance. After all, this was one of the most favorite plays by Menander, read through-

65 We have not been able to trace an arbitration scene in the visual arts of late antique Egypt. Outside Egypt the most conspicuous example is the famous third century A.D. mosaic from the "House of Menander" at Mytilene on Lesbos. According to the inscription that accompanies the mosaic, it portrays the arbitration scene from the second act of the *Epitrepontes* of Menander, from which the play took its title. The standard edition of the mosaic is S. Charitonidis, L. Kahil, & R. Ginouvès, *Les mosaïques de la maison du Ménandre á Mytilène* (Berne, 1970) 44 ff. and plate 4.

66 See the introduction to the *editio princeps* of the plays: G. Lefebvre, *Fragments d'un manuscrit de Ménandre* (Cairo, 1907). That codex, which came to be known as the Cairo Codex, contained substantial parts of the comedies *Heros, Epitrepontes, Periciromene,* and *Samia* as well as unidentified fragments.

out the Roman world precisely because of the arbitration scene. According to the advice given by the Roman professor of forensic oratory Quintilian in the second century A.D., the *Epitrepontes* served as a model for the kind of judicial oratory needed in everyday practice at the bar in Rome.[67] The *Epitrepontes* is the first among the plays of Menander that Quintilian highlights. Although the legal system of fourth century B.C. Athens was radically different from that of early imperial Rome, Quintilian apparently saw no problem in giving this piece of advice. By the sixth century the legal system of Rome had been exported to the rest of the Roman empire, and the kind of needs of students of forensic oratory Quintilian addressed had also become urgent in the eastern part of the empire, including Egypt. Thanks to imperial legislation, legal training had become uniform throughout the empire. Rhetorical training was thoroughly integrated with the legal training of those who, like Dioscorus,[68] were involved with the practical side of the law: the notaries and the *scholastikoi*. The Attic orators of the fourth century B.C., especially Isocrates, were their models in producing their own legal discourse. Isocrates was admired by Dioscorus, as we have seen in section 4. The notaries and *scholastikoi* also embellished their texts with bon mots derived from the comedies of Menander, either directly or through collections of these bon mots (the so-called *Sententiae Menandreae*).[69] These collections were part and parcel of the ordinary school curriculum.

The dispute between the clergymen we referred to at the beginning of this section (**#15**) was eventually settled through mediation by two *scholastikoi*. These are the late antique version of the forensic orators Quintilian advised to study Menander. We now know that Quintilian's advice did not go unheeded more than four centuries after he gave it. What might have surprised Quintilian is that his advice was applicable

67 See Quintilian, *Inst.* X 1, 69-71. The only demonstration of the aptness of Quintilian's advice is that given reluctantly by J.W. Cohoon, "Rhetorical Studies in the Arbitration Scene of Menander's Epitrepontes," *TAPA* 45 (1914): 141-230. Cohoon shows that a rhetorical reading of this scene in its fourth century B.C. context is possible, but he does not discuss the kind of rhetorical reading Quintilian envisaged in the context of the early Roman empire.

68 For Dioscorus' own involvement in arbitration, see L.S.B. MacCoull, op. cit. (note 20 above) 22-23 (a Coptic arbitration document drawn up by Dioscorus himself) and 36-47 (on *P.Lond.* V 1709).

69 For Dioscorus' use of these bon mots, see L.S.B. MacCoull, op. cit. (note 20 above) 79.

to such a distant and hardly Romanized part of the Roman empire as Egypt. In hindsight we can add that by the sixth century A.D. the Mediterranean shared a common cultural heritage to a far greater degree than had ever been the case before. The need for a "common denominator" was recognized by the late antique state and was addressed by favorable policies.

10. *The legal-anthropological context*

The term legal anthropology has usually been reserved for the study of law in primitive societies with no codified legal tradition whatsoever. A legal-anthropological approach is, however, also very helpful in studying legal documents from more developed societies. Private settlements are prime source material for this kind of approach. They allow insights into the functioning of society and the distribution of power within the community. Settlements renegotiate and therefore explicate the various social and economic relations that exist between disputants, such as family relations, power relations, and the ownership of property. Let us first give an overview of the material for late antique Egypt.

As we have pointed out already, our document is a well preserved private settlement from late antiquity. In terms of length and details it is surpassed only by its contemporaries **#20** and **#41**. The latter document identifies itself as a so-called *stipulatio Aquiliana,* a settlement according to Roman law, mentioned a few times in the Digest.[70] The Greek and Coptic examples of this type of contract preserved on papyrus have been scrutinized by previous scholars for their information about the legal practices of late antiquity.[71] The material has since grown quite substantially. In the list on pp. 121-7 we have collected all the published Greek[72] texts from late antique Egypt that are more or less certainly

---

70 See F. Sturm, *Stipulatio Aquiliana. Textgestalt und Tragweite der aquilianischen Ausgleichsquittung im klassischen römischen Recht* (Munich, 1972). Sturm examines the late antique examples on pp. 44-48.

71 See especially the article by A. Steinwenter, "Das byzantinische Dialysis-Formular," *Studi Aldo Albertoni,* Vol. 1 (Padua, 1935): 73-97.

72 A small fragment of an unpublished sixth century Greek *dialysis* is mentioned in *P.Sarga,* p. 15. The likewise unpublished P.Mich.inv. 4008 (A.D. 364) contains an unusual *dialysis* from the Small Oasis relating to the distribution of state land, the so-called *epinemesis* (forthcoming in *ZPE*).

agreements of settlement. We have excluded texts relating to divorce agreements, which are also sometimes called *dialyseis* (e.g., *SB* VI 9278), because a recent study has been devoted to this topic.[73] Likewise, we have not taken into consideration Coptic settlements from Thebes, because all of these postdate the Arab conquest.[74] There are numerous other texts that somehow relate to arbitration, disputes and settlements,[75] such as the so-called *amerimneiai* or indemnities, in Greek as well as in Coptic.[76] The subject deserves a more detailed treatment from the point of view of legal history than is available at present.[77]

---

73 See R.S. Bagnall, "Church, State and Divorce in Late Roman Egypt," *Florilegium Columbianum* (New York, 1987): 41-61.

74 They have been subjected to close scrutiny by W.C. Till, *Erbrechtliche Untersuchungen aufgrund der koptischen Urkunden* (Wien, 1953) 14-27. We have been able to trace three Coptic *dialyseis* that are not from Thebes and apparently predate the Arab conquest. Unfortunately they are rather fragmentary: *P.Ryl.copt.* 183 and 184 as well as *BKU* III 353. *P.Lond.* IV 1587, 1595, 1599, and 1611 are fragmentary Coptic *dialytikai homologiai* from Aphrodito that postdate the Arab conquest. *P.Lond.* IV 1599 once refers to itself as a *dialal[etike homologia.*

75 *P.Oxy.* LIV 3757, 19 (A.D. 325) refers to τὸ γραμματεῖον τῆϲ μεταξὺ γενομένηϲ διαλύϲεωϲ. The editor thinks (p. 144) that the document referred to is *P.Oxy.* LIV 3756 (325), which, however, calls itself an ἀποτελεστικὴ ἀποχή ("final receipt"). The prefect had ordered the two parties to settle their dispute. *P.Oxy.* XXII 2352 (5th century A.D.) might relate to a settlement, but seems to come from a record of proceedings. *P.Cair.Masp.* II 67166 (from Antinoopolis; 568) is an *akyrosia* ("annulment" or "cancellation"), but it casually calls itself a *dialytike homologia* once. *P.Cair.Masp.* II 67156 (from Antinoopolis; 570) is a contract between a mother and her daughter, but it is not certain that it is the settlement of a dispute. *P.Köln ägypt.* 17 (7th century A.D.) is a letter proposing a private settlement through negotiation or, if this is not acceptable, arbitration by "a godly man." *P.Grenf.* I 65 (6th/7th century A.D.) is an idiosyncratic document difficult to classify on any count.

76 For a case of the latter, see the text published by M. Krause, "Ein Fall friedensrichtlicher Tätigkeit im ersten Jahrzehnt des 7. Jhdts. im Oberägypten," *RdÉ* 24 (1972): 101-07. Two Coptic *amerimneiai* or indemnities, which do not come from Thebes, are *BKU* I 53 and *CPR* IV 111 (from Hermopolis; 7th century A.D.).

77 For the Ptolemaic and early Roman periods, see the references in R. Taubenschlag, *The Law of Greco-Roman Egypt in the Light of the Papyri* (2d ed. Warsaw, 1955) 403-406. For an even earlier period, see A. Steinwenter, *Die Streitbeendigung durch Urteil, Schiedsspruch und Vergleich nach griechischem Rechte* (Munich, 1925).

We want to discuss two topics here: the social context of settling disputes in late antiquity and the preference for private settlements to the virtual exclusion of all other forms of dispute processing. We feel that we cannot ignore the wider context, especially now that private settlements have come to the attention of social historians interested in the family in other periods.[78] Because an anthropology of late antique law by itself is impossible, we want to concentrate on the actual process by which people settled their disputes in a social context. How did they manipulate laws, rules, customs, and principles to get the best deal they could–without unduly damaging the relationships that existed between them? This question involves the two dynamic factors influencing the disputing process in general.[79] On the one hand there is the predicament, the object of dispute. On the other hand there is the constraint, the relationship between the parties. The choice of action depends on how the predicament correlates to the constraint in the minds of the disputants. They may aim more at securing the disputed object than at salvaging the relationship between them. But at the same time their relationship itself varies and this in turn will have an impact on their choice of action. They can decide to involve only that part of their relationship that directly relates to the dispute, e.g., the fact that they are the buyer and seller of a piece of property. But they can also decide to involve their wider relationships, e.g., the fact that they are from the same village or even from the same family. And we also have to allow for developments over time; one party can change its mind after the other has made a move.

To figure all this out for late antique Egypt is extremely difficult, because the documents for all their prolixity are often reluctant to give details about how the dispute arose and developed until the time of settlement itself, who initiated the settlement in the first place, how the mediators were chosen, what motives dictated the actions of the parties and how these changed over time. Transactional modes and tactical strategies are hardly visible in the texts. In the list on pp. 121-7 we have made this kind of information explicit as best we could. A good number of texts explicitly refer to a course of action preceding the settlement,

---

78 Foremost Th. Kuehn, *Law, Family, and Women: Towards a Legal Anthropology of Renaissance Italy* (Chicago, 1991), especially pp. 1-126 and 176-93.

79 The following is based on J.L. Comaroff & S. Roberts, *Rules and Processes: The Cultural Logic of Dispute in an African Context* (Chicago, 1981) 115-17. This book is concerned with dispute processing among the South African tribe of the Tswana, but the authors carefully distinguish between what is peculiar to this tribe and what belongs to their own model.

such as a petition to an official (see **#2, #4, #7, #9, #10, #12, #14** , and **#15**) or even joinder of issue (see **#3** and **#5**). **#20** is a striking text in that it gives a long narrative of the actions undertaken by the parties. One of them, Psaius, makes three independent moves to complicate the case. The first two are rebutted as irrelevant or dismissed because of the lapse of time. The third move, although strictly unrelated to the issue at hand, is incorporated in the final agreement, because the other party is somehow involved.[80] This is a clear case where the parties decided to involve the wider relationships between them.

A large number of settlements on papyrus (see **#4, #6, #19, #23, #25, #26 , #27, #29, #30**, and **#35**) relate to family disputes over inherited property, which involve the whole spectrum of relationships between disputants.[81] The preponderance of family disputes is a natural consequence of the fact that the transmission of property in late antiquity occurs to a large degree within families. Even when a will exists,[82] the death of an older generation creates a power vacuum among the heirs, who have to reconfigure the ownership of the property among themselves. This also explains why women are often involved as owners of a share of the disputed property. It has been argued[83] that inheritance of real estate by women became more common in Egypt in the Roman period because of the growing importance of private landownership, and

---

80 The other party is represented by the priest Victor, the son of Dioscorus' uncle Besarion, and Senuthes, Dioscorus' brother. The third move of Psaius relates to what Apollos, presumably Dioscorus' father, did to Psaius long ago. As the text informs us, Apollos had died 19 years before the events relating to the final stage of the settlement. The date of the document therefore should be about A.D. 564/565. The editor's identification of one of the witnesses, Apollos son of Dioscorus, with the father of the notary Dioscorus cannot be correct. We think that the Apollos mentioned here is the son of the notary Dioscorus.

81 For a discussion of **#23, #25, #26, #27** and **#29** , see J.J. Farber, "Family Disputes in the Patermouthis Archive," *BASP* 27 (1991): 111-22.

82 In the period from A.D. 300 to 700 wills are very scarce. Scholars have tried to justify this scarcity by arguing that people in the late period preferred the use of "paratestamentary" documents such as *donationes inter vivos* or *mortis causa*. The most recent discussion and a summary of the arguments is in R.S. Bagnall, "Two Byzantine Legal Papyri in a Private Collection," *Studies Arthur Schiller* (Leiden, 1986): 1-9.

83 By D.W. Hobson, "Women as Property Owners in Roman Egypt," *TAPA* 113 (1983): 311-21.

this remains so in the later period. Women are highly visible in family disputes over the division of inheritances in Roman and late antique Egypt. Apart from kinship relations, the settlements also reflect wider social relationships, such as that between neighbors with adjoining property or between partners in trade (e.g., **#10**) or between master and journeyman (e.g., **#28**). Other forms of property, such as money and all sorts of movables, as well as minor criminal offenses, such as petty theft (again **#28**), are much more exceptional objects of dispute.

If we knew in all instances which party suggested the settlement first and where that party was located in the social spectrum, we would be able to explain the forces governing the outcome of the settlements. It is not unlikely that the distribution of power within the community was somehow reflected in the outcome of the settlements. The weaker party in social terms would seem to stand a better chance in an informal setting than in the courts, which were dominated by the peers of the stronger parties in social terms. This seems to be exemplified by **#20**, 40-49, where we read in the editor's translation:

> Pleading against this the people of the prosecuting party proved that they had often used loud complaints in the Holy Church against John of discreet memory and that they also often had approached the official at the head of the district regarding this reason but that after there had been much cajolery by the opponents the discussion about that enquiry had been closed.

The weaker party, here identified as "the prosecuting party," had used a church service as the setting for their public protest against the clergyman John–no doubt to make sure witnesses were present.[84] They also tried to initiate legal proceedings with the help of the official mentioned. Even though John must have been embarrassed when he was booed in his own church, he was able to hush up the issue through his connections with those in power. After the death of John the weaker party tried to break through the impasse by offering John's heirs a private settlement.

---

84 *P.Lond.* I 77 (p. 234), 45-46 explicitly excludes public protest in church as a means of redress. That the John of **#20** was a clergyman follows from the use of the adjective *eulabes* to characterize him. See on this O. Hornickel, *Ehren- und Rangprädikate in den Papyrusurkunden. Ein Beitrag zum römischen und byzantinischen Titelwesen* (Giessen, 1930) 13-14. That he was the priest of the main church of Aphrodito is suggested by the fact that his heirs are represented by the current priest of that Church, Victor.

Unfortunately, the texts do not always support such a simple scenario as the one implied by **#20**. In a few cases the party initiating the settlement indeed seems to be the weaker party in social terms (in addition to **#20** see **#9, #12, #28**, and **#29**), but, as far as we can tell, in as many cases the party initiating the settlement is the stronger party in social terms (see **#11, #15, #16, #32**, and **#41**). Moreover, in many instances we cannot detect a social difference between the parties at all, and even if we could, the majority of cases deal with the kind of people one would not call the peers of the ruling élite dominating the local courts at all. The more likely assumption is that in the majority of cases the party with the weaker case initiated the settlement, to get at least something out of it, rather than losing out completely in a court of law where stricter rules of justice were applied.

It has been noted that settlements out of court seem to proliferate in late antiquity.[85] The number of private settlements increases over time and they become the preferred option of solving disputes to the virtual exclusion of all other options. In the Ptolemaic and early Roman periods there is some evidence for private settlements too,[86] and one of the main reasons why we know more about them is the increased visibility of the actual documents recording private settlements in late antiquity compared to the earlier period. From the third century A.D. onwards private settlements are recorded in a special type of text, no doubt under the influence of Roman law.[87] Earlier on private settlements were recorded differently, e.g., in a cession of land, if that were the disputed property, with no reference to the dispute that preceded.

The preference for private settlements as a means for solving disputes could be a byproduct of the codification of Roman law in late antiquity. This not only enhanced the visibility of law, but also created a growing demand for specialized legal knowledge. Apart from going to

---

85 Most recently by A.A. Schiller, op. cit. (note 64 above) 469-502.

86 E.g., *P.Mert.* II 59 (154 or 143 B.C.), *BGU* VI 1249 (148/147 B.C.) and *P.Tor.Choach.* 9 (126 B.C.), where settlements are reached after a petition had been filed by one of the disputing parties. *P.Fam.Tebt.* 20 (A.D. 120) is a petition to cancel a legal action after the disputing parties have reached an agreement (*dialysis*).

87 In our view late antique *dialyseis* are an innovation *in form* of the Roman period. There are of course many similarities *in substance* with private settlements of earlier periods. We think S. Allam, "Observations on Civil Jurisdiction in Late Byzantine and Early Arabic Egypt," *Life in a Multi-cultural Society: Egypt from Cambyses to Constantine and Beyond* (Chicago, 1992): 1-8 confuses form and substance.

court disputants could now also avail themselves of the services of the legal specialists of the age, the notaries and lawyers, to manipulate these rules to the satisfaction of both parties. This explains the form that most of the settlements take, i.e., notarial documents, as well as the prolific use in such documents of legal formulas derived from published laws. We have discussed this at some length in our section 8.

Private settlements may thus have become an attractive option to solve disputes in addition to the other available options, but this does not explain why they seem to have put the courts out of business altogether. There is hardly any positive evidence for the use of the courts to settle disputes after about A.D. 500.[88] In the settlements listed on pp. 121-7 courts are mentioned in a negative formula, in which the courts as an alternative way to solve the dispute are explicitly rejected, as in our text (lines 63-64).[89] In some instances, as we have seen, preliminary court proceedings[90] or petitions[91] requesting such proceedings precede the settlement of a dispute out of court. Until the end of the fifth century many private settlements thus came about with the help of an official. Presumably, this official suggested to the parties that they settle their dispute privately.[92] Even this more or less informal involvement of officials[93] seems almost to disappear from the record after the end of the fifth century.

---

88 See, e.g., E. Seidl, "Die Jurisprudenz ägyptischer Provinzialrichter byzantinischer Zeit," *Festschrift Ernst Rabel*, Vol. 2 (Tübingen, 1954): 235-61.

89 A.A. Schiller, op. cit. (note 64 above) 493 comments: "The clause in which a party agreed not to dispute 'in court or out of court' must have signified in the sixth/seventh century an agreement not to engage in controversy by any manner of means."

90 See also **#29**, a case involving an official at an early stage of the settlement. He may or may not have acted in his official capacity.

91 See also D. Simon, "Zur Zivilgerichtsbarkeit im spätbyzantinischen Ägypten," *RIDA* III 18 (1971): 651-52.

92 For a parallel from tenth-century Cairo, see S.D. Goitein, *A Mediterranean Society: The Jewish Communities of the Arab World as Portrayed in the Documents of the Cairo Geniza*, Vol. 2 (Berkeley, 1978) 335.

93 Contrast the role of officials implied in the early Ptolemaic period by *P.Enteux.*, where the lower officials are ordered by their superior to settle the dispute mentioned in the petition (see the recurring formula μάλιστα διάλυσον αὐτούς).

It has been suggested that the references to courts in the texts just referred to are fictitious altogether.[94] According to this theory there were no courts to try civil cases in late antique Egypt at all. Disputes like the ones dealt with in the private settlements could not have been settled in court at all. The theory could even put the criminal courts out of business, because some of the cases dealt with in the settlements are not "civil" cases in our sense of the term. There is a case of petty theft (**#28**). Of course, one cannot really argue from a case such as this that there were no criminal courts. There may have been special circumstances (unknown to us) which led to settlement. However, the fact that cases such as theft were not taken to court underscores the marginal role of courts even in matters that the law recognizes as criminal. The Egyptians in late antiquity favored an approach based on personal relationships when it came to solving problems between members of their community and especially their family. After the Arab conquest the evidence for Egyptians taking recourse to courts becomes stronger again. The theory of the absence of civil courts in late antique Egypt, however, cannot stand.[95] Evidence for the *physical* presence of civil courts comes from texts that are as late as ours.[96] The early Arabic papyri include citations to court, petitions and requests for legal advice relating to (potential) lawsuits, very much alike the early Roman evidence.[97] In other words, the situation in late antique (i.e. Christian, not pagan or islamic) Egypt is substantially different from that in the early Roman and the early Islamic period and therefore requires an explanation.

In explaining the preference for private settlements over other options to solve disputes we have to take other factors into account. One

---

94 By A.A. Schiller, op. cit. (note 64 above) 469-502.

95 Schiller's arguments have been thoroughly refuted by D. Simon, op. cit. (note 91 above) 623-57. Simon lists a number of other options available to, but hardly ever used by, disputants, such as the rescript procedure, which had to be arranged in Constantinople (see our note on line 65 in the commentary). Obviously such an option was too expensive to be considered by most Egyptians, who did not have the time or leisure to go to Constantinople.

96 See the note to line 9 in our commentary. In *P.Princ.* II 82, 13, of A.D. 427, a *mega dikasterion* is mentioned in a civil matter and this cannot be anything but a real courthouse because of the adjective.

97 The early Islamic evidence has been assessed by G. Frantz-Murphy, "Settlement of Property Disputes in Provincial Egypt: Early Islamic Period," *al-Masâq. Studia Arabo-Islamica Mediterranea* 6 (1993): 95-105.

factor is the complexity of the legal procedures. It was also more costly and time-consuming to go to court. If one had to wait until a judge pronounced a verdict to take possession of some disputed property such as land, it might be too late for sowing it. Both the distress caused by a court procedure and the costs of the trial are actually mentioned as reasons for settling a dispute privately in *SB* III 7033, 29, where one of the parties to a dispute, a bishop, is said not to be able to bear the hardship of the courts (*dikastike diagymnasia*), and in **#41**, 41-42, where it is bluntly stated that, in addition to the danger of losing the case in a court of law, one must also cover the fees of the judges (εὐλαβούμενοϲ μὴ πρὸϲ τῇ τοιαύτῃ τῆϲ δίκηϲ ϲυντριβῇ ζημιωθῇ καὶ τοὺϲ μιϲθοὺϲ τῶν δικαϲτῶν).

There is reason to assume that things in Egypt were the same as elsewhere.[98] In that case we cannot ascribe the preference for private settlements to the dislike Egyptian "monophysite" Christians supposedly felt for the imperial government and its institutions, including the civil courts. Thoroughly "orthodox" Christians elsewhere preferred private settlements too. We do not think that there was such a dislike for the imperial government among Egyptian Christians and vice versa.[99] After all, there were emperors, such as Anastasius, who were openly practicing monophysites. At least, in the settlements from late antique Egypt no such sentiments are ever referred to. It is very difficult to extract from the texts anything remotely resembling rules, customs, and principles of this sort, which must have somehow informed the decisions made by the disputing parties during the settlement process. But that does not mean that the Egyptians of late antiquity lived in an amoral universe. In other historical societies scholars have also found that the texts are often silent when it comes to principles behind the decisions made.[100]

---

98 There is no evidence for other parts of the Roman empire, but the legal texts do not seem to offer a radically different picture from the papyri. The legal texts simply concentrate on the court procedures, whereas the papyri tend to illustrate settlements out of courts. For the civil courts in late antiquity, see D. Simon, *Untersuchungen zum justinianischen Zivilprozess* (Munich, 1969).

99 A.A. Schiller, op. cit. (note 64 above) 500-502 presents this idea along with other platitudes about late antique Egypt that need no refutation here.

100 See, e.g., W. Davies, "Disputes, Their Conduct and Their Settlement in the Village Communities of Eastern Brittany in the Ninth Century," *History and Anthropology* 1 (1985): 289-312. Her database for ninth-century Brittany consists of about forty settlements (p. 295) just as ours.

Because we cannot, like modern ethnographers, ask our "subjects" to provide structured narratives about their decisions or tell us about the motives behind their actions, we are left with a very indirect way of reconstructing these motives. Just as we invoked the evidence from a literary text (Menander's *Epitrepontes*) to illustrate the background of arbitration and mediation in late antique Egypt in section 9, we now briefly explore the evidence from New Testament passages referring explicitly to settlements of disputes. The New Testament influenced the moral universe of late antique Egyptians. In the numerous churches the New Testament was read aloud to the congregation, and if they were not booing the priest (as in **#20**), those present would listen and allow the texts to shape their moral principles. After several centuries of Christianity in Egypt the message had presumably rooted deeply in the minds of the majority of the population. A typical passage from a gospel is Luke 12: 57-59 (cf. Matthew 5: 25-26), which reads in the New Revised Standard Version:

> And why do you not judge for yourselves what is right? Thus, when you go with your accuser before a magistrate, on the way make an effort to settle the case, or you may be dragged before the judge, and the judge hand you over to the officer, and the officer throw you in prison. I tell you, you will never get out until you have paid the very last penny.

All the elements that we have been discussing are present in this text: the dispute, the initiated court proceedings, the private settlement before the actual lawsuit takes place, and the reasons to prefer private settlement of disputes over the services of government institutions. First and foremost among these reasons is the personal relationship between two close acquaintances, who also happen to be co-religionists. This is what we have previously called the constraint imposed upon the settlement of a dispute by the web of relationships in which the disputants are entwined. As additional reasons for settling disputes privately Luke mentions the negative consequences of involving a government institution: prison sentence and a complete failure to win the case. A private settlement is less risky and allows both parties to get at least something out of the deal. This is what we have previously called the predicament in which the disputants find themselves. They have to decide whether their goal is to get what they think they deserve and to run the risk of losing it all, or whether they should salvage their ties with one another as much as possible. In a private settlement the parties are bound to strike some sort of deal. A government official, on the other hand, might decide to give one of the parties the upper hand.

In the earlier Roman period petitions to initiate a lawsuit in the case of a dispute are far more frequent than the kind of settlements we are discussing here.[101] It has been suggested[102] that petitions are more frequently used in stratified communities in Egypt, such as nome capitals, whereas private settlements are more frequently found in unstratified communities, such as villages. This suggestion is not corroborated by our evidence for late antique Egypt, where all settlements with the possible exception of those from Aphrodito and the greater Theban area (**#35**) come from nome capitals. No civil lawsuit is on record for these cities, only a few petitions initiating such a lawsuit, and even these petitions were canceled afterwards by a private settlement.

Lawsuits and private settlements are useful as complementary options to solve a dispute. As we have seen before, there are cases in late antique Egypt where a private settlement was preceded by joinder of issue or a petition. In the earlier Roman period, a petition could be addressed to any level of the administrative officialdom.[103] It seems very likely that in some instances (such as **#15**) these two means were used as leverage by one of the parties to make sure that a private settlement would turn out more favorably for them. It seems as if the bishop in **#15** was brought to his knees by the fact that his deacon filed a petition against him with the prefect. Only then he consented to mediation and a settlement. On the other hand, settlements did not necessarily bring the case to a successful end. It may have taken multiple attempts at settlements to put an end to an extremely complicated dispute, as seems to be the case in **#41**.

A settlement once concluded could also be disputed at a later time. To prevent this, settlements contained stipulations about fines (the *epitimia* to be paid to the government and the *prostimon* to be paid to the

---

101 See D.W. Hobson "The Impact of Law on Village Life in Roman Egypt," in *Law, Politics and Society* (Sheffield, Engl., 1993): 193-219. Her database of 182 petitions of the earlier Roman period includes 143 instances of disputes (p. 203).

102 By R.S. Bagnall, "Official and Private Violence in Roman Egypt," *BASP* 26 (1989): 201-16.

103 For the earlier period D.W. Hobson argues that "the petition to an official for help in settling a local dispute is actually the end of the disputing process rather than the beginning," op. cit. (note 101 above) 199. This seems to be reversed in the later period.

other party) to be paid in case of breach of contract.[104] We can tell that this was felt to be an important part of the settlement, because in our text "the laws" are mentioned only in relation to the *epitimia* (line 87). With this stipulation the disputants involved the government as a potentially interested party–without notifying any government institution before the need to do so arose. The frequency with which we encounter stipulations about fines–some high, some low–suggests that even this clause did not always deter people from breaking a settlement. It is remarkable how rarely the settlements refer to laws, rules, customs, and principles other than in the context of these fines. In our text other legal institutions are mentioned in lines 65-66, such as *ad hoc* imperial legislation, but only to pronounce them irrelevant to the case at hand. The outside world is kept out completely and the boundaries of the town are the confines of the settlement. Even when the dispute is settled outside these boundaries, as in our text, the matter is solved in the presence of members of the same community. The world of the settlements is carefully construed as a small world of local proportions.

To conclude: as we have seen on pp. 38-39 many settlements are made between close relatives. The subject matter of these settlements is property inherited from a deceased parent. The survivors have to work out an agreement over the division of the property. Settlements in general are therefore part of the rites of passage enacted by the relatives at the death of a parent. The ritual not only involves the burial of the deceased, but also the redistribution of their property and power. What we have in the documents is only the outcome of this particular rite of passage, the final agreement about the property left by the deceased. Settlements are products of a string of social events (dispute, negotiation, mediation or arbitration). As historians of late antique Egyptian society we have only these final products. Those who were directly responsible for putting such documents in writing, the notaries such as Dioscorus, do not paint a static picture of their small world but record a series of rites of passage.

11. *How to proceed from here*

Our text ultimately derives its interest from the perspective it offers on how real people settled their disputes with one another almost fifteen

---

104 See our notes on lines 84 and 87 in the commentary.

centuries ago. We feel that a document like this has too often been treated as repetitive and tautologous and therefore undeserving of more general study.[105] That is why we have commented on the document at such great length. In the footsteps of the editors of *P.Münch.* and indeed of those of the late antique scribes themselves a document like this deserves detailed discussion, as a whole and in its parts (see lines 80-81). We hope to have shown that a satisfactory picture of settling disputes in late antique Egypt is only possible if we take the social context into account. This helps us ask questions that lead to a better understanding of the world of late antiquity.

We would like to conclude this introduction with an anecdote taken from an anthropological study that deals with a village in modern Crete:[106]

> The police also know that an attitude of respect for local norms constitutes a far greater asset than their status as the representatives of a resented legal system. Occasionally, they learn the hard way. A non-Cretan police officer obstinately insisted on going up into the foothills alone to arrest a suspected sheep thief, ignoring the [villagers]' advice to take a couple of local mediators with him. As he approached the *mitato* (stone-built shepherds' hut) where the suspect was hiding, the latter dashed out and started to run away at great speed. The officer drew his service revolver and took aim. The suspect's elderly crippled father, fearing for the life of his son, suddenly hurled himself at the officer and beat him senseless with his stick, snatched up the officer's uniform cap and revolver, and hastily disappeared. The officer eventually regained consciousness and crawled painfully back down to the village, where he was given first aid as well as a stern homily on the importance of listening to local advice and custom. After a suitably admonitory delay, his cap and revolver were restored to him. Upon recovery, he applied for a transfer, and at the same time lodged a formal complaint with the local court. When the case finally came up for adjudication, the judge asked the suspected sheep thief's father to stand up. The old man did so. Was *this* the [villager] who had so badly mauled the healthy young

105 Much in the vein of H. Zilliacus, *Zur Abundanz der spätgriechischen Gebrauchssprache* (Helsinki, 1967).

106 M. Herzfeld, *The Poetics of Manhood: Contest and Identity in a Cretan Mountain Village* (Princeton, 1985) 26-27.

> police officer? Assured that indeed it was, he dismissed the case amidst derisive laughter.

As historians of late antique Egypt we are as unfamiliar with its society as the policeman in the story was with that of Crete. We have to come to terms with the society of late antique Egypt if we want to avoid the fate of the policeman.

Reading Text and Translation

Reading Text

Date

[lost, but probably equivalent to ca. A.D. 537]

Address (1a-5)

Αὐρήλιος Νικαντίνοος Ἰσιδώρου συντελεστὴς ἀπὸ κώμης Ἀφροδίτης | διάγων ἐνταῦθα ἐπὶ τῆς Ἀντινοέων καλλιπόλεως Αὐρηλίοις Φοιβάμμωνι | Τριαδέλφου καὶ αὐτῷ συντελεστῇ καὶ τῇ τούτου γαμετῇ Ἀναστασίᾳ τῇ καὶ | Τεκρομπίᾳ θυγατρὶ Μεγάλου ὁρμωμένοις ἀπὸ τῆς αὐτῆς κώμης Ἀφροδίτης | διὰ σοῦ Ἀπολλῶτος Διοσκόρου πρωτοκωμήτου τῆς εἰρημένης κώμης θείου σου [5] τῆς προγεγραμμένης Ἀναστασίας πρὸς μητρὸς χαίρειν.

Agreement proper (i): *general statement by Nicantinous* (5-6)

ὁμολογῶ ὑμῖν | τὰ ἑξῆς ὑποτεταγμένα·

Translation

Date

[lost, but probably ca. A.D. 537]

Address (1a-5)

"Aurelius Nicantinous, son of Isidorus, collective taxpayer from the village of Aphrodito, who resides here in the fair city of the Antinoites, to the Aurelii Phoebammon, son of Triadelphus, who is also a collective taxpayer, and Anastasia alias Tecrompia, his wife, daughter of Megas, who come from the same village of Aphrodito, represented by you, Apollos, son of Dioscorus, chief of the said village, uncle of you, the [5] aforementioned Anastasia, on your mother's side, greetings.

Agreement proper (i): *general statement by Nicantinous* (5-6)

I acknowledge to you the following:

Agreement proper (ii): *background of the case* (6-28)

(a) *Facts* (6-17): ἐγὼ ὁ προγεγραμμένοϲ Νικαντίνοοϲ ϲυντελεϲτὴϲ | διάλυϲιν ϲυνεθέμην καθ’ ὑμῶν τῶν προγεγραμμένων Φοιβάμμωνοϲ καὶ | Ἀναϲταϲίαϲ τῆϲ αὐτῆϲ γαμετῆϲ διὰ ϲοῦ τοῦ προλεχθέντοϲ Ἀπολλῶτοϲ | πρωτοκωμήτου ἐν τῷ κατὰ χώραν πολιτικῷ δικαϲτηρίῳ περὶ τοῦ χρέουϲ [10] ὡϲανεὶ καταβληθέντοϲ παρ’ ἐμοῦ τὸ τηνικαῦτα ὑπὲρ λυτρώϲεωϲ | ὑποθήκηϲ γεγενημένηϲ παρὰ τῶν αὐτοῦ γονέων εἰϲ ὄνομα Ἰωϲηφίου | υἱοῦ ὑπὲρ τοῦ κτήματοϲ ὑποτεθέντοϲ αὐτῷ παρὰ τῶν ἐμῶν γονέων | καὶ διαπραθέντοϲ ὑμῖν τοῖϲ προγεγραμμένοιϲ Φοιβάμμωνι καὶ | Ἀναϲταϲίᾳ τῇ αὐτοῦ γαμετῇ παρὰ τῶν ἐμῶν ἀδελφιδῶν πρὸ ὀλίγου [15] χρόνου, φημὶ δὴ Εὐδοξίαϲ καὶ Ἀντωνίαϲ καὶ Κολλούθου, ἀκολούθωϲ | τῇ δυνάμει τῶν γεγενημένων ὑμῖν παρ’ αὐτῶν πράϲεων τοῦ αὐτοῦ | κτήματοϲ τῶν καὶ τὴν ἰδίαν ἰϲχὺν ἐχουϲῶν.

(b) *Arbitration* (17-28): καὶ πολλῶν εἰρημένων καὶ | κινηθέντων μεταξὺ ἐμοῦ Νικαντινόου καὶ Ἀπολλῶτοϲ πρωτοκωμήτου | ἐπὶ τὰ ἐνταῦθα τοῦ καὶ ἀναπληροῦντοϲ τὴν χώραν ὑμῶν τῶν προ[20]γεγραμμένων πρὸ δίκηϲ καὶ πρὸ διαγνωϲτικῶν ἀγώνων τέλοϲ φίλοι | ἀγαθοὶ μέϲοι ἡμῶν γενόμενοι διαλαβόντεϲ τὰ τοῦ πράγματοϲ | ἐδικαίωϲαν ἐμὲ τὸν αὐτὸν Νικαντίνοον λαβεῖν παρ’ ὑμῶν ὑπὲρ πάϲηϲ | ἀπαλλαγῆϲ τοῦ καταβληθέντοϲ παρ’ ἐμοῦ χρέουϲ εἰϲ λύτρωϲιν ὑποθήκηϲ | τοῦ προειρημένου κτήματοϲ χρυϲοῦ νομίϲματα ἑπτὰ ἕκαϲτον [25] παρὰ κεράτια δύο τῷ χρυϲοχοϊκῷ ϲταθμῷ τῆϲ εἰρημένηϲ κώμηϲ | Ἀφροδίτηϲ καὶ ϲίτου ἀρτάβαϲ εἴκοϲι πενταμέτρῳ τῷ μέτρῳ ϲου | τοῦ αὐτοῦ Φοιβάμμωνοϲ τοῦ τὴν τάξιν ὑμῶν τῶν προγεγραμμένων | ἀναπληροῦντοϲ.

Agreement proper (ii): *background of the case* (6-28)

(a) *Facts* (6-17): I, the aforementioned Nicantinous, collective taxpayer, made a settlement with regard to you, the aforementioned Phoebammon and Anastasia, the said wife, represented by you, the aforesaid Apollos, village chief, in the local civil courthouse with regard to the debt [10] that has now indeed been paid by me for the redemption of a deed of security drawn up in favor of Iosephius, the son, on the initiative of his parents concerning the estate that was put up as security for him by my parents and that was sold to you, the aforementioned Phoebammon and Anastasia, his wife, by my nephew and nieces a short [15] while ago, that is to say Eudoxia and Antonia and Colluthus, in accordance with the legal force of the deeds of sale of the said estate that have been drawn up by them for you and that are valid on their own.

(b) *Arbitration* (17-28): And after many words have been said and many moves have been made here between me, Nicantinous, and Apollos, village chief and the one who represents you, the aforementioned [20], finally, before a lawsuit and before cognition trials took place, good friends mediated between us by taking up the case, they decided that I, the said Nicantinous, for the complete discharge of the debt, paid by me to redeem the deed of security over the aforesaid estate, receive from you seven gold solidi [25] each minus two carats according to the goldsmiths' standard of the said village of Aphrodito and twenty artabas of wheat according to the five-measures standard that belongs to you, the said Phoebammon as the representative of the two of you, the aforementioned.

Agreement proper (iii): *terms and conditions* (28-81)

τούτων τοίνυν οὕτω γενομένων καὶ ϲτερχθέντων καὶ | ἀρεϲθέντων ἐμοί τε Νικαντινόῳ καὶ Ἀπολλῶτι πρωτοκωμήτῃ πρὸϲ τὴν κρίϲιν τῶν μέϲων φίλων τούτου ἕνεκα εἰϲ ταύτην ἐλήλυθα | τὴν ἔγγραφον διαλυτικὴν ὁμολογίαν δι' ἧϲ ὁμολογῶ ἐγὼ ὁ προγεγραμ|μένοϲ Νικαντίνοοϲ ἑκουϲίᾳ γνώμῃ καὶ προαιρέϲει ἰδίᾳ ἀμετανοήτῳ καὶ | ἀδόλῳ βουλήϲει, ὀρθῇ διανοίᾳ δίχα δόλου παντὸϲ καὶ φόβου καὶ βίαϲ καὶ | ἀπάτηϲ καὶ ἀνάγκηϲ

(a) *Receipt of payment* (34-40): εἰληφέναι μὲν καὶ πεπληρῶϲθαι παρ' ὑμῶν τῶν προγεγραμμένων Φοιβάμμωνοϲ καὶ Ἀναϲταϲίαϲ διὰ ϲοῦ τοῦ προ|λεχθέντοϲ Ἀπολλῶτοϲ πρωτοκωμήτου τὰ δόξαντα δίδοϲθαί μοι | πρὸϲ τὴν δικαίαν κρίϲιν τῶν μέϲων φίλων, τουτέϲτιν νομίϲματα | ἑπτὰ παρὰ κεράτια δεκατέϲϲαρα καὶ ϲίτου ἀρτάβαϲ εἴκοϲι πενταμέτρῳ, | πρὸϲ τὸ ἐμὲ ἀπ' ἐντεῦθεν ἤδη ἀναδοῦναί ϲοι τὴν αὐτὴν ὑποθήκην εἰϲ ἀκύρωϲιν,

(b) *Renunciation of claims* (40-51): μηδένα δὲ λόγον ἔχειν ἢ ἕξειν πρὸϲ ὑμᾶϲ καὶ κληρονόμουϲ | ὑμῶν καὶ διαδόχουϲ καὶ διακατόχουϲ, μὴ πρὸϲ τὸν αὐτὸν Ἀπολλῶν | καὶ τοὺϲ αὐτοῦ κληρονόμουϲ, – οὐκ ἐγώ, οὐ κληρονόμοι μου, οὐ διάδοχοι, | οὐ διακάτοχοι – μὴ περὶ τοῦ αὐτοῦ χρέουϲ τοῦ καταβληθέντοϲ παρ' ἐμοῦ | τὸ τηνικαῦτα Ἰωϲηφίῳ εἰϲ λύτρωϲιν τοῦ αὐτοῦ κτήματοϲ, μὴ περὶ τῆϲ εἰρημένηϲ ὑποθήκηϲ, μὴ περὶ νομῆϲ ἢ δεϲποτείαϲ τοῦ προ|ειρημένου κτήματοϲ τοῦ διακειμένου ἐν πεδιάδι τῆϲ αὐτῆϲ κώμηϲ | Ἀφροδίτηϲ ἐν κλήρῳ καλουμένῳ Μουνλακον ἐκ νότου τῆϲ ὁδοῦ | τῆϲ βαλλούϲηϲ ἐπὶ τὴν κώμην Τμονεχθη, μὴ περὶ προϲόδων τούτου, | μὴ περὶ οἱουδήποτε πράγματοϲ ἀνήκοντοϲ τῷ αὐτῷ κτήματι δικαίῳ ἢ μὴ ἀνήκοντοϲ, μικροῦ ἢ μεγάλου, ἐγγράφου ἢ ἀγράφου, ἀκρίτου ἢ | κεκριμένου τὸ ϲύνολον,

Agreement proper (iii): *terms and conditions* (28-81)

Because these things, then, have taken place in this way and we are content and pleased with them, both I, Nicantinous, and Apollos, village chief, [30] because of this and in accordance with the judgment of the mediating friends, I have proceeded to this written agreement of settlement through which I, the aforementioned Nicantinous, acknowledge of my own free will and by my own irrevocable choice and with honest intent, of sound mind, without any fraud and without fear and force and deceit and compulsion,

(a) *Receipt of payment* (34-40): on the one hand that I have received and have been paid in full by you, the [35] aforementioned Phoebammon and Anastasia, represented by you, the aforesaid Apollos, village chief, that what has been agreed upon to be given to me in accordance with the fair judgment of the mediating friends, i.e., seven solidi minus fourteen carats and twenty artabas of wheat according to the five-measures standard, in order that from this very moment I hand over to you the said deed of security [40] for cancellation,

(b) *Renunciation of claims* (40-51): and on the other hand that I have or will have no claim against you and your heirs and successors and their substitutes by default, nor against the said Apollos and his heirs, – neither I nor my heirs or successors nor their substitutes by default, – neither with regard to the said debt, which has now been paid by me to Iosephius for the redemption of the said estate, nor with regard to [45] the said deed of security, nor with regard to the possession or ownership of the aforementioned estate located in the plain of the said village of Aphrodito in the lot called Mounlakon south of the road that leads to the village of Tmonechthe, nor regarding its proceeds, nor regarding anything whatsoever that belongs to the said estate by legal right [50] or does not belong to it, small or large, written or unwritten, adjudicated altogether or not.

(c) *Confirmation of ownership* (51-57): ἀλλ' ἔχειν ὑμᾶϲ δεϲποτικῷ δικαίῳ ἐπὶ τὸ | διηνεκὲϲ τὴν νομὴν καὶ τὴν δεϲποτείαν τοῦ προειρημένου κτήματοϲ | μετὰ παντὸϲ αὐτοῦ τοῦ δικαίου διὰ τὸ ἐμὲ εἰληφέναι ἐκ πλήρουϲ | τὰ δόξαντα δίδοϲθαί μοι παρ' ὑμῶν διὰ ϲοῦ τοῦ προλεχθέντοϲ Ἀπολλῶτοϲ, τουτέϲτιν νομίϲματα ἑπτὰ παρὰ κεράτια δεκατέϲϲαρα | χρυϲοχοϊκῷ ϲταθμῷ τῆϲ εἰρημένηϲ κώμηϲ καὶ ϲίτου ἀρτάβαϲ | εἴκοϲι πενταμέτρῳ,

(d) *Settlement proper* (57-76): καὶ ἀπηλλάχθαι καὶ διαλελύϲθαι πρὸϲ ὑμᾶϲ ἐν ἅπαϲι | καὶ μηδεμίαν μοι τοῦ λοιποῦ ϲῴζεϲθαι καθ' ὑμῶν οἱανδήποτε ἀγωγὴν | εἰϲ πρόϲωπον ἢ καὶ εἰϲ πρᾶγμα ἁρμόϲαϲαν ἢ καὶ ἁρμόϲαι δυναμένην ἐκ παντὸϲ τοῦ προλαβόντοϲ χρόνου μέχρι τῆϲ ϲήμερον καὶ προ|γεγραμμένηϲ ἡμέραϲ καὶ εἰϲ τὸν ἑξῆϲ ἅπαντα καὶ διηνεκῆ χρόνον καὶ | μὴ δύναϲθαί μέ ποτε καιρῷ ἢ χρόνῳ ἐγκαλεῖν ὑμῖν καὶ τοῖϲ ὑμῶν | κληρονόμοιϲ ἐν δικαϲτηρίοιϲ καὶ ἐκτὸϲ δικαϲτηρίων – ἐπιχωρίῳ | ἢ ὑπερορίῳ – μὴ δι' ἐμοῦ, μὴ δι' ἐντολέωϲ, μὴ διὰ παρενθέτου προϲώπου ἢ θείαϲ φιλοτιμίαϲ ἢ πραγματικοῦ τύπου ἢ ῥεϲκρίπτου ἢ θείου | νεύματοϲ ἢ δικανικῆϲ λεπτολογίαϲ ἢ ἑτέραϲ οἱαϲδήποτε αἰτίαϲ | ϲυμβῇ ταύτην ἀτονῆϲαι ἢ μέροϲ αὐτῆϲ, ἀλλὰ καὶ ἐϲβέϲθαι μοι | καθ' ὑμῶν καὶ κατὰ τῶν ὑμῶν κληρονόμων οἱανδήποτε ἀγωγὴν | εἰϲ πρόϲωπον ἢ εἰϲ πρᾶγμα ὡϲ ἀνωτέρω εἴρηται διὰ τὸ μηδεμίαν μετουϲίαν ἔχων τοῦ λοιποῦ πρὸϲ ὑμᾶϲ περί τε τοῦ αὐτοῦ κτήματοϲ | ἢ περὶ νομῆϲ τούτου ἢ περὶ χρέουϲ ἢ περὶ ἑτέρου τινὸϲ πράγματοϲ | ἀνήκοντοϲ τῷ αὐτῷ κτήματι καὶ παντὸϲ αὐτοῦ δικαίου τὸ ϲύνολον | διὰ τὸ ἐμὲ εἰληφέναι ἐκ πλήρουϲ τὰ δόξαντα δίδοϲθαί μοι πρὸϲ | τὴν κρίϲιν τῶν μέϲων φίλων, τουτέϲτιν νομίϲματα ἑπτὰ παρὰ κεράτια δεκατέϲϲαρα χρυϲοχοϊκῷ ϲταθμῷ καὶ ϲίτου ἀρτάβαϲ εἴκοϲι ὡϲ πολλάκιϲ | εἴρηται.

(c) *Confirmation of ownership* (51-57): but (I acknowledge) that you have by legal right of ownership forever the possession and the ownership of the aforesaid estate with every legal right that belongs to it, because I have received in full what has been agreed upon to be given to me by you represented by you, the aforesaid [55] Apollos, i.e., seven solidi minus fourteen carats according to the goldsmiths' standard of the said village and twenty artabas of wheat according to the five-measures standard,

(d) *Settlement proper* (57-76): and (I acknowledge) that I have been released and am settled with you on all points and that from now on no legal action whatsoever is left for me against you, either personally or with regard to your property, whether the action is fitting or can be made to fit, [60] from all preceding time until the present and above-mentioned day and for all subsequent and everlasting time; and (I acknowledge) that I am not able at any moment or time to proceed against you or your heirs in courts of law, be they local or elsewhere, or out of court, neither I on my own, nor through an authorized representative, nor through a man of straw, [65] irrespective of whether this (acknowledgment) or part of it might become ineffective on the basis of an imperial munificence or an imperial decree or a rescript or an imperial will or a juridical argument or on whatever other basis; but (I acknowledge) that any legal action whatsoever against you and against your heirs, either personally or with regard to property, has been extinguished for me, as it was said above, because I have no [70] part with you from now on with regard to the said estate or with regard to its possession or with regard to the debt or with regard to whatever other thing that may belong to the said estate and every legal right that belongs to it altogether, because I have received in full what has been agreed upon to be given to me in accordance with the judgment of the mediating friends, i.e., seven solidi minus [75] fourteen carats according to the goldsmiths' standard and twenty artabas of wheat, as has often been said.

Agreement proper (iv): *oath sworn in the name of the emperor* (76-81)

καὶ προϲεπὶ τούτοιϲ πᾶϲι καὶ ἐφ' ἑκάϲτῳ τῶν προγεγραμμένων | κεφαλαίων ἐπωμοϲάμην τήν τε ἁγίαν καὶ ὁμοούϲιον τριάδα καὶ | τὴν εὐϲέβειαν καὶ νίκην τοῦ καλλινίκου δεϲπότου τῆϲ οἰκουμένηϲ | Φλαουίου Ἰουϲτινιανοῦ τοῦ αἰωνίου αὐγούϲτου αὐτοκράτοροϲ ἐμμένειν διηνεκῶϲ τῇ δυνάμει ταύτηϲ τῆϲ διαλυτικῆϲ ὁμολογίαϲ καὶ | παντὶ μέρει αὐτῆϲ καὶ κεφαλαίῳ καὶ κατὰ μηδένα τρόπον παραβῆναι. |

Agreement proper (v): *penalty clause* (82-96)

εἰ δέ ποτε καιρῷ ἢ χρόνῳ τολμήϲαιμι παραβῆναι πάντα τὰ διομολο|γηθέντα παρ' ἐμοῦ ἐν ταύτῃ τῇ διαλυτικῇ ὁμολογίᾳ καὶ βουληθείην | ὑπεναντίον τι χωρεῖν, ὁμολογῶ παραϲχεῖν ὑμῖν λόγῳ προϲτίμου ἐπὶ μόνου τοῦ ἐπιχειρήματοϲ τῆϲ παραβάϲεωϲ χρυϲοῦ νομιϲμάτια | εἰκοϲιτέϲϲαρα ἔργῳ καὶ δυνάμει ἀπαιτούμενα πρὸϲ τῷ ὑποκεῖϲθαί με | τῷ τῆϲ ἐπιορκείαϲ κινδύνῳ καὶ τοῖϲ ὡριϲμένοιϲ κατὰ νόμουϲ ἐπιτιμίοιϲ | κατὰ τῶν παραβαίνειν ἐπιχειρούντων τὰϲ ἐνωμότουϲ ἑαυτῶν ϲυνθήκαϲ, | οὐδὲν δὲ ἧττον καὶ πρὸ τοῦ προϲτίμου καὶ μετὰ τὴν τοῦ προϲτίμου καταβολήν, εἴ ποτε πρὸϲ ἀπαίτηϲιν ἁρμόϲοι, ἀρραγῆ καὶ ἀϲάλευτον εἶναι ταύτην | τὴν διαλυτικὴν ὁμολογίαν διὰ παντὸϲ ἥνπερ ὑμῖν ἐθέμην | πρὸϲ ἀϲφάλειαν κυρίαν οὖϲαν καὶ βεβαίαν ὑποθέμενοϲ ὑμῖν | εἰϲ ἅπαντα τὰ προγεγραμμένα καὶ εἰϲ τὴν τοῦ προϲτίμου ἀπαίτηϲιν, | εἰ οὕτω τύχοι, πάντα τὰ νῦν ὄντα μοι καὶ ἐϲόμενα πράγματα κινητά τε καὶ ἀκίνητα καὶ αὐτοκίνητα ἐνεχύρου λόγῳ καὶ ὑποθήκηϲ | δικαίῳ καθάπερ ἐκ δίκηϲ·

Agreement proper (iv): *oath sworn in the name of the emperor* (76-81)

And for all this in general and for each one of the aforementioned items separately I took an oath by the holy and consubstantial Trinity and the piety and victory of the gloriously triumphant lord of the world, Flavius Justinianus, the eternal august emperor, that I abide [80] forever by the legal force of this agreement of settlement and to each of its parts and items and that I will not transgress it in any way.

Agreement proper (v): *penalty clause* (82-96)

And if at any moment or time I should dare to transgress all the things agreed upon by me in this agreement of settlement, and if I should ever want to proceed contrary to it in any way, I acknowledge that I will give to you as a fine [85] for the mere attempt at transgression twenty-four gold solidi, to be demanded as a matter of fact and with full legal power, apart from being subject to the risk of perjury and to the penalties stipulated by the laws against those who attempt to transgress their own sworn agreements, and that nonetheless both before and after the payment of the fine, [90] if anyone ever sets out to make a demand, this acknowledgment of settlement shall be unbroken and unshaken forever, and I have executed it for your safety, being valid and guaranteed, while I put up as security for you with regard to all the aforementioned and with regard to the demand of the fine, if that should be the case, all that I now own and shall own, movables [95] and immovables and self-movables, as a pledge and with the legal right of security, as if ruled by court;

Agreement proper (vi): *clause validating the agreement* (96-98)

καὶ εἰϲ τὰ προγεγραμμένα πάντα | ἐπερωτηθεὶϲ παρ' ὑμῶν ταῦθ' οὕτωϲ ἔχειν, δώϲειν, ποιεῖν, φυλάττειν, | ἐμμένειν, πληρώϲειν, εἰϲ πέραϲ ἄγειν ὡμολόγηϲα.

Signatures and subscription (98-116)

(2d hand) Αὐρήλιοϲ Νικαντίνοοϲ | Ἰϲιδώρου ὁ προγεγραμμένοϲ ἐθέμην ταύτην τὴν διαλυτικὴν ὁμολογίαν ἐϲχηκὼϲ ἐκ πλήρουϲ τὰ δόξαντα, τουτέϲτιν | νομιϲμάτια ἑπτὰ καὶ ϲίτου ἀρτάβαϲ εἴκοϲι, καὶ ὤμοϲα | τὸν θεῖον ὅρκον ἐπὶ τῷ προϲτίμῳ καὶ πείθωμαι πᾶϲι τοῖϲ | ἐγγεγραμμένοιϲ ὡϲ πρόκειται καὶ ὑπογράψαϲ ἀπέλυϲα.

(3d hand) Αὐρήλιοϲ | Μουϲῆϲ Ψαίου ϲυντελεϲτὴϲ ἀπὸ τῆϲ αὐτῆϲ κώμηϲ Ἀφροδίτηϲ εὑρεθεὶϲ ἐν Ἀντινόου μαρτυρῶ τῇ ὁμολογίᾳν ἤτοι διαλύϲει | ἀκούϲαϲ παρὰ τοῦ θεμένου.

(4th hand) Ἑρμαῶϲ Βόττου ἀπὸ τῆϲ αὐτῆϲ | κώμηϲ Ἀφροδίτηϲ εὑρεθεὶϲ ἐν Ἀντινόου μαρτυρῶ τῇ | διαλυτικῇ ὁμολογίᾳ ἀκούϲαϲ παρὰ τοῦ θεμένου.

(5th hand) Αὐρήλιοϲ | Ϲενούθηϲ Ἀπολλῶτοϲ ἀπὸ τῆϲ αὐτῆϲ κώμηϲ Ἀφροδίτηϲ εὑρεθεὶϲ ἐν Ἀντινόου μαρτυρῶ τῇ διαλυτικῇ ὁμολογίᾳ ἀκούϲαϲ παρὰ τοῦ θεμένου. |

Agreement proper (vi): *clause validating the agreement* (96-98)

and having been asked the formal question by you regarding all the aforementioned, I have acknowledged that this is so, that I shall give it, that I do it, keep it, abide by it, that I shall fulfill it, that I bring it to an end.

Signatures and subscription (98-116)

(2d hand) "I, Aurelius Nicantinous, son of Isidorus, the aforementioned, have made this [100] agreement of settlement after having received in full the amount agreed upon, i.e., seven solidi and twenty artabas of wheat, and I took the imperial oath regarding the fine and I agree with all that is written in it above, and after having signed it I have released it."

(3d hand) "I, Aurelius Muses, son of Psaius, collective taxpayer from the said village of Aphrodito, [105] currently in Antinoopolis, am witness to the agreement or settlement after having heard it from the man who made it."

(4th hand) "I, Hermaos, son of Bottus, from the said village of Aphrodito, currently in Antinoopolis, am witness to the agreement of settlement, after having heard it from the man who made it."

(5th hand) "I, Aurelius Senuthes, son of Apollos, from the said village of Aphrodito, currently [110] in Antinoopolis, am witness to the agreement of settlement after having heard it from the man who made it."

(6th hand) Αὐρήλιοc Ἀπολλῶc Βηcίου ἀπὸ τῆc αὐτῆc κώμηc Ἀφροδίτηc εὑρεθεὶc | ἐν Ἀντινόου μαρτυρῶ τῇ διαλυτικῇ ὁμολογίᾳ ἀκούcαc παρὰ τοῦ θεμένου. |

(7th hand) . . . ἀκούcαc παρὰ τοῦ θεμένου.

(illegible traces of three more lines; the last line must have contained the signature of the notary)

(6th hand) "I, Aurelius Apollos, son of Besius, from the said village of Aphrodito, currently in Antinoopolis, am witness to the agreement of settlement after having heard it from the man who made it."

(7th hand) ". . . after having heard it from the man who made it."

(illegible traces of signatures of one or two more witnesses and the subscription of the notary)

Transcription of the Greek Text

[ ]	lacuna on the papyrus
( )	resolution of an abbreviation
⟨ ⟩	omission by the scribe
{ }	superfluously written text
` ´	interlinear addition
α̣β̣γ̣δ̣	uncertain letters
....	illegible letters

P.Vat.Aphrod. 10 + P.Mich.inv. 6922

Antinoopolis — ca. A.D. 537

Physical description: originally the papyrus consisted of nine sheets fastened together to make a roll; each sheet was about 30 cm wide and 20 cm high. The papyrus was rolled up from the bottom. The first sheet is now incomplete at the top, because it was on the outside. The back of the Vatican piece is blank. The same is true for the Michigan piece except that some ink from the text on the front has left mirror images on the back. The ink was still wet when the papyrus was rolled up for the first time and, as a result, it left these traces. The text is written *transversa charta*, i.e., across the fibers in one long column, as are almost all the larger legal documents of later date. Cf. E.G. Turner, *The Terms Recto and Verso. The Anatomy of the Papyrus Roll* (Brussels, 1978) 47-50. The writing of the body of the text is practiced and almost calligraphic and is comparable to that of another, contemporary, settlement also drawn up in Antinoopolis, **#20**. The hands of the individual signatures at the bottom are described at appropriate places in the commentary.

[date]

a [† Αὐρήλιος Νικαντίνοος Ἰσιδώρου συντελεστὴς ἀπὸ κώμης Ἀφροδίτης]

1 διάγων ἐνταῦθα ἐπὶ τῆς Ἀντινοέων καλλιπόλεως Α̣ὐ̣ρ̣η̣λί̣ο̣[ις]

Φ̣[οιβά]μ̣μ̣[ωνι]

2 Τριαδέλφου καὶ αὐτῷ συντελεστῇ καὶ τῇ τούτου γαμετῇ Ἀναστασίᾳ τῇ καὶ

3 Τεκρομπίᾳ θυγατρὶ Μεγάλου ὁρμωμένοις ἀπὸ τῆς αὐτῆς κώμης Ἀφροδίτης

4 διὰ σοῦ Ἀπολλῶτος Διοσκόρου πρωτοκωμήτου τ̣ῆς εἰρημένης κώμης θείου

σου

1. διάγων J. Gascou, *Aegyptus* 61 (1981) 278: διὰ τῶν ed.princ. Αὐρηλίῳ ed.princ.

4. πρωτοκωμήτου corr. from πρωτοκομήτου

[τ]ῆ̣[ϲ προγ]εγραμμένηϲ Ἀναϲταϲίαϲ π̣ρὸϲ μητρὸϲ χαίρ(ειν). ὁμολογῶ ὑμῖν [τὰ ἑξῆϲ ὑποτ]εταγ̣μ̣ένα· ἐγὼ ὁ προγεγραμμένοϲ Νικαντίνοοϲ ϲυντελεϲτὴϲ διά̣λ[υ]ϲ̣ι[ν ϲ]υ̣ν̣εθέμην καθ' [ὑμῶν τῶν] προγεγραμμένων Φοιβάμμωνοϲ καὶ Ἀναϲταϲίαϲ τῆϲ αὐτῆϲ γαμετῆϲ διὰ ϲοῦ τοῦ προλεχθέντοϲ Ἀπολλῶτοϲ πρωτοκομήτου ἐν τῷ κατὰ χώραν πολιτικῷ δικαϲτηρίῳ περὶ τοῦ χρέουϲ ὡ̣ϲανεὶ καταβληθέντοϲ παρ' ἐμοῦ τὸ τηνικαῦτα ὑπὲρ λυτρώϲεωϲ [ὑ]π̣[ο]θήκηϲ γεγενημένηϲ παρὰ τῶν αὐτοῦ γονέων εἰϲ ὄνομα Ἰωϲηφίου [υἱοῦ ὑπὲ]ρ τοῦ κτήματοϲ ὑποτεθέντοϲ αὐτῷ παρὰ τῶν ἐμῶν γονέων κ̣[αὶ διαπ]ραθέντοϲ ὑμῖν τοῖϲ προγεγραμμένοιϲ Φοιβάμμωνι καὶ Ἀναϲταϲίᾳ τῇ αὐτοῦ γαμετῇ παρὰ τῶν ἐμῶν ἀδελφιτῶν πρὸ ὀλίγου χρόνου, φημὶ δὴ Εὐδοξίαϲ καὶ Ἀντωνίαϲ καὶ Κολλούθου, ἀκολούθωϲ τῇ δυνάμει τῶν γεγενημένων ὑμῖν παρ' αὐτῶν πράϲεων τοῦ αὐτοῦ κ̣τήματοϲ τῶν καὶ τὴν ἰδίαν ἰϲχὺν ἐχουϲῶν. καὶ πολλῶν εἰρημένων καὶ κινηθέντων μεταξὺ ἐμοῦ Νικαντινόου καὶ Ἀπολλῶτοϲ πρωτοκωμήτου ἐπὶ τὰ ἐνταῦθα τοῦ καὶ ἀναπληροῦντοϲ τὴν χώραν ὑμῶν τῶν προγεγραμμένων πρὸ δίκηϲ καὶ πρὸ διαγνωϲτικῶν ἀγώνων τέλοϲ φίλοι ἀγαθοὶ μέϲοι ἡμῶν γενόμενοι {οἵτινεϲ} διαλαβόντεϲ τὰ τοῦ πράγματοϲ ἐδικαίωϲαν ἐμὲ τὸν αὐτὸν Νικαντίνοον λαβεῖν παρ' ὑμῶν ὑπὲρ πάϲη[ϲ] [ἀ]παλλαγῆϲ τοῦ καταβληθέντοϲ παρ' ἐμοῦ χρέουϲ εἰϲ λύτρωϲιν ὑποθήκηϲ τοῦ προειρημένου κτήματοϲ χρυϲοῦ νομίϲματα ἑπτὰ ἕκαϲτον παρὰ κεράτια δύο τῷ χρυϲοχοϊκῷ ϲταθμῷ τῆϲ εἰρημένηϲ κώμηϲ

7. α̣λ̣ . . . . [ ]̣ . . . θ̣εμην καθ` [c. 13] ed.princ. καθ' corr. from κατ' 9. read πρωτοκωμήτου 10. Π̣τ̣ανει ed.princ. ὕπερ pap. 11. ϊωϲηφιου pap. 12. [c. 4 ὑπέ]ρ ed.princ. ὕποτεθεντοϲ pap. 13. μεταπ]ραθέντοϲ ed.princ. ὕμιν pap. 14. read ἀδελφιδῶν 16. ὕμιν pap. 17. ϊδιαν ϊϲχυν pap. 18. πρωτοκωμήτου corr. from πρωτοκομήτου 19. ὕμων pap. 22. ὕμων ὕπερ pap. 23. ὕποθηκηϲ pap. 24. ἑκάϲτου ed.princ. 25. χρυϲοχοϊκω pap.

26 Ἀφροδίτηϲ καὶ ϲίτου ἀρτάβαϲ εἴκοϲι πενταμέτρῳ τῷ μέτρῳ ϲου
27 τοῦ αὐτοῦ Φοιβάμμωνοϲ τοῦ τὴν τάξιν ὑμῶν τῶν προγεγραμμένων
28 ἀ̣ν̣[α]π̣ληροῦντοϲ. τούτων τοίνυν οὕτω γενομένων καὶ ϲτερχθέντων καὶ
29 ἀρεϲθέντων ἐμοί τε Νικαντινόῳ καὶ Ἀπολλῶτι πρωτοκωμήτῃ
30 πρὸϲ τὴν κρίϲιν τῶν μέϲων φίλων τούτου ἕνεκα εἰϲ ταύτην ἐλήλυθα
31 τὴν ἔγγραφον διαλυτικὴν ὁμολογίαν δι' ἧϲ ὁμολογῶ ἐγὼ ὁ προγεγραμ-
32 μένοϲ Νικαντίνοοϲ ἑκουϲίᾳ γνώμῃ καὶ προαιρέϲει ἰδίᾳ ἀμετανοήτῳ καὶ
33 ἀδόλῳ βου̣λήϲει, ὀρθῇ διανοίᾳ δίχα δόλου παντὸϲ καὶ φόβου καὶ βίαϲ καὶ
34 ἀπάτηϲ καὶ ἀνάγκηϲ εἰληφέναι μὲν καὶ πεπληρῶϲθαι παρ' ὑμῶν τῶν
35 προγεγραμμένων Φοιβάμμωνοϲ καὶ Ἀναϲταϲίαϲ διὰ ϲοῦ τοῦ προ-
36 λεχθέντοϲ Ἀπολλῶτοϲ πρωτοκωμήτου τῶν δοξάντων δίδοϲθαί μοι
37 πρὸϲ τὴν δικαίαν κρίϲιν τῶν μέϲων φίλων, τουτέστιν νομίϲματα
38 ἑπτὰ παρὰ κεράτια δεκατέϲϲαρα καὶ ϲίτου ἀρτάβαϲ εἴκοϲι πενταμέτρῳ,
39 πρὸϲ τῷ ἐμὲ ἀπ' ἐντεῦθεν ἤδη ἀναδοῦναί ϲοι τὴν αὐτὴν ὑποθήκην
40 εἰϲ ἀκύρωϲιν, μηδένα δὲ λόγον ἔχειν ἢ ἕξειν πρὸϲ ὑμᾶϲ καὶ κληρονόμουϲ
41 ὑμῶν καὶ διαδόχουϲ καὶ διακατόχουϲ, μὴ πρὸϲ τὸν αὐτὸν Ἀπολλῶν
42 καὶ τοὺϲ αὐτοῦ κληρονόμουϲ, οὐκ ἐγώ, οὐ κληρονόμοι μου, οὐ διάδοχοι,
43 οὐ διακάτοχοι μὴ περὶ τοῦ αὐτοῦ χρέουϲ τοῦ καταβληθέντοϲ παρ' ἐμοῦ
44 τὸ τηνικαῦτα Ἰωϲηφίῳ εἰϲ λύτρωϲιν τοῦ αὐτοῦ κτήματοϲ, μὴ περὶ
45 τῆϲ εἰρημένηϲ ὑποθήκηϲ, μὴ περὶ νομῆϲ ἢ δεϲποτείαϲ τοῦ προ-
46 ειρημένου κτήματοϲ τοῦ διακειμένου ἐμ πεδιάδι τῆϲ αὐτῆϲ κώμηϲ
47 Ἀφροδίτηϲ ἐν κλήρῳ καλούμενον Μουνλακον ἐκ νότου τῆϲ ὁδοῦ

26. ϋμων pap. 29. πρωτοκωμήτῃ corr. from πρωτοκομήτῃ space filler at the end of line 32. ϊδια pap. 34. ϋμων pap. 35. πρωτοκωμήτου corr. from πρωτοκομήτου 36. read τὰ δόξαντα 39. read τό ϋποθηκην pap. 40. ϋμαϲ pap. 41. ϋμων pap. 42. ουὶ pap. 44. ϊωϲηφιω pap. 45. ϋποθηκηϲ pap. 46. read ἐν 47. read καλουμένῳ; horizontal bar over Μουνλακον

48 τῆϲ βαλλούϲηϲ ἐπὶ τὴν κώμην Τμονεχθη, μὴ περὶ προϲόδων τούτου,
49 μὴ περὶ οἱουδήποτε πράγματοϲ ἀνήκοντοϲ τῷ αὐτῷ κτήματι δικαίῳ
50 ἢ μὴ ἀνήκοντοϲ, μικροῦ ἢ μεγάλου, ἐγγράφου ἢ ἀγράφου, ἀκρίτου ἢ
51 κεκριμένου τὸ ϲύνολον, ἀλλ' ἔχειν ὑμᾶϲ δεϲποτικῷ δικαίῳ ἐπὶ τὸ
52 διηνεκὲϲ τὴν νομὴν καὶ τὴν δεϲποτείαν τοῦ προειρημένου κτήματοϲ
53 μετὰ παντὸϲ αὐτοῦ τοῦ δικαίου διὰ τὸ ἐμὲ εἰληφέναι ἐκ πλήρουϲ
54 τὰ δόξαντα δίδοϲθαί μοι παρ' ὑμῶν διὰ ϲοῦ τοῦ προλεχθέντοϲ
55 Ἀπολλῶτοϲ, τουτέϲτιν νομίϲματα ἑπτὰ παρὰ κεράτια δεκατέϲϲαρα
56 χρυϲοχοϊκῷ ϲταθμῷ τῆϲ εἰρημένηϲ κώμηϲ καὶ ϲίτου ἀρτάβαϲ
57 εἴκοϲι πενταμέτρῳ, καὶ ἀπηλλάχθαι καὶ διαλελύϲθαι πρὸϲ ὑμᾶϲ ἐν ἅπαϲι
58 καὶ μηδεμίαν μοι τοῦ λοιποῦ ϲῴζεϲθαι καθ' ὑμῶν οἱανδήποτε ἀγωγὴν
59 εἰϲ πρόϲωπον ἢ \`καὶ´ εἰϲ πρᾶγμα ἁρμοϲάϲηϲ ἢ καὶ ἁρμόϲοι δυναμένηϲ
60 ἐκ παντὸϲ τοῦ προλαβόντοϲ χρόνου μέχρι τῆϲ ϲήμερον καὶ προ-
61 γεγραμμένηϲ ἡμέραϲ καὶ εἰϲ τὸν ἑξῆϲ ἅπαντα καὶ διηνεκῆ χρόνον καὶ
62 μὴ δύναϲθαί μέ ποτε καιρῷ ἢ χρόνῳ ἐγκαλεῖν ὑμῖν καὶ τοῖϲ ὑμῶν
63 κληρονόμοιϲ ἐν δικαϲτηρίοιϲ καὶ ἐκτὸϲ δικαϲτηρίων ἐπιχωρίῳ
64 ἢ ὑπερορίῳ μὴ δι' ἐμοῦ, μὴ δι' ἐντολέωϲ, μὴ διὰ παρενθέτου προϲώπου
65 ἢ θείαϲ φιλοτιμίαϲ ἢ πραγματικοῦ τύπου ἢ ῥεϲκρίπτου ἢ θείου
66 νεύματοϲ ἢ δικανικῆϲ λεπτολογίαϲ ἢ ἑτέραϲ οἱαϲδήποτε αἰτίαϲ
67 ϲυμβῇ ταύτην ἀτονῆϲαι ἢ μέρουϲ αὐτῆϲ, ἀλλὰ καὶ ἐϲβέϲθαι μοι
68 καθ' ὑμῶν καὶ κατὰ τῶν ὑμῶν κληρονόμων οἱανδήποτε ἀγωγὴν
69 εἰϲ πρόϲωπον ἢ εἰϲ πρᾶγμα ὡϲ ἀνωτέρω εἴρηται διὰ τὸ μηδεμίαν
70 μετουϲίαν ἔχων τοῦ λοιποῦ πρὸϲ ὑμᾶϲ περί τε τοῦ αὐτοῦ κτήματοϲ

48. horizontal bar over Τμονεχθη 51. αλλ\` pap. ϋμαϲ pap. 54. ϋμων pap. 56. χρυϲοχοϊκω pap. 57. ϋμαϲ pap. 58. καθ\` ϋμων pap. 59. read ἁρμόϲαϲαν ἢ καὶ ἁρμόϲαι δυναμένην 62. ϋμιν pap. ῡμων pap. 64. ϋπερορ ιω pap. 67. read μέροϲ 68. καθ\` ϋμων και κατα των ϋμων pap. 70. ϋμαϲ pap.

ἢ περὶ νομῆϲ τούτου ἢ περὶ χρέουϲ ἢ περὶ ἑτέρου τινὸϲ πράγματοϲ ἀνήκοντοϲ τῷ αὐτῷ κτήματι καὶ πᾶν αὐτοῦ δίκαιον τὸ ϲύνολον διὰ τὸ ἐμὲ εἰληφέναι ἐκ πλήρουϲ τὰ δόξαντα δίδοϲθαί μοι πρὸϲ τὴν κρίϲιν τῶν μέϲων φίλων, τουτέϲτιν νομίϲματα ἑπτὰ παρὰ κεράτια δεκατέϲϲαρα χρυϲοχοϊκῷ ϲταθμῷ καὶ ϲίτου ἀρτάβαϲ εἴκοϲι ὡϲ πολλάκιϲ εἴρηται. καὶ προϲεπὶ τούτοιϲ πᾶϲι καὶ ἐφ' ἑκάϲτῳ τῶν προγεγραμμένων κεφαλαίων ἐπωμοϲάμην τήν τε ἁγίαν καὶ ὁμοούϲιον τριάδα καὶ τὴν εὐϲέβειαν καὶ νίκην τοῦ καλλινίκου δεϲπότου τῆϲ οἰκουμένηϲ Φλ(αουίου) Ἰουϲτινιανοῦ τοῦ αἰωνίου αὐγούϲτου αὐτοκράτοροϲ ἐμμένειν διηνεκῶϲ τῇ δυνάμει ταύτηϲ τῆϲ διαλυτικῆϲ ὁμολογίαϲ καὶ παντὶ μέρει αὐτῆϲ καὶ κεφαλαίῳ καὶ κατὰ μηδένα τρόπον παραβῆναι. εἰ δέ ποτε καιρῷ ἢ χρόνῳ τολμήϲαιμι παραβῆναι πάντα τὰ διομολογηθέντα παρ' ἐμοῦ ἐν ταύτῃ τῇ διαλυτικῇ ὁμολογίᾳ καὶ βουληθείην ὑπεναντίον τι χωρεῖν, ὁμολογῶ παραϲχεῖν ὑμῖν λόγῳ προϲτίμου ἐπὶ μόνου τοῦ ἐπιχειρήματοϲ τῆϲ παραβάϲεωϲ χρυϲοῦ νομιϲμάτια εἰκοϲιτέϲϲαρα ἔργῳ καὶ δυνάμει ἀπαιτούμενα πρὸϲ τῷ ὑποκεῖϲθαί με τῷ τῆϲ ἐπιορκίαϲ κινδύνῳ καὶ τοῖϲ ὡριϲμένοιϲ κατὰ νόμουϲ ἐπιτιμίοιϲ κατὰ τῶν παραβαίνειν ἐπιχειρούντων τὰϲ ἐνωμότουϲ ἑαυτῶν ϲυνθήκαϲ, οὐδὲν δὲ ⟨ἧττον⟩ καὶ πρὸ τοῦ προϲτίμου καὶ μετὰ τὴν τοῦ προϲτίμου καταβολήν, εἴ ποτε πρὸϲ ἀπαίτηϲιν ἁρμόϲοι, ἀρραγῆ καὶ ἀϲάλευτον εἶναι ταύτην τὴν διαλυτικὴν ὁμολογίαν διὰ παντὸϲ ἥνπερ ὑμῖν ἐθέμην

72. read παντὸϲ αὐτοῦ δικαίου 75. χρυϲοχοϊκω pap. 77. ἐπωμοϲάμην corr. from ἐπωμόϲαμεν 78. above καλλινίκου traces of writing 79. φλS ϊουϲτινιανου pap. 84. ϋπεναντιον pap. ϋμιν pap. 85. ϋπερ pap. 86. ϋποκειϲθαι pap. 87. read ἐπιορκείαϲ 88. κατά written in the left margin 90. ἁρμόϲοι corr. from ἁρμόϲαι 91. ϋμιν pap.

92 πρὸc ἀcφάλειαν κυρίαν οὖcαν καὶ βεβαίαν ὑποθέμενοc ὑμῖν
93 εἰc ἅπαντα τὰ προγεγραμμένα καὶ εἰc τὴν τοῦ προcτίμου ἀπαίτηcιν,
94 εἰ οὕτω τύχοι, πάντα τὰ νῦν ὄντα μοι καὶ ἐcόμενα πράγματα κινητά τε
95 καὶ ἀκίνητα καὶ αὐτοκίνητα ἐνεχύρου λόγῳ καὶ ὑποθήκηc
96 δικαίῳ καθάπερ ἐκ δίκηc· καὶ εἰc τὰ προγεγραμμένα πάντα
97 ἐπερωτηθεὶc παρ' ὑμῶν ταῦθ' οὕτωc ἔχειν, δώcειν, ποιεῖν, φυλάττειν,
98 ἐμμένειν, πληρώcειν, εἰc πέραc ἄγειν ὡμολόγηcα. † (2d hand) † Αὐρήλιοc
Νικαντίνοοc
99 Ἰcιδώρου ὁ προγεγραμμένοc ἐθέμην ταύτην τὴν διαλυτικὴν
100 ὁμολογίαν ἐ`c´χηκὸc ἐκ πλήρουc τὰ δόξαντα, τουτέcτιν
101 νομιcμάτια ἑπτὰ καὶ cίτου ἀρτάβαc εἴκοcει, καὶ ὄμιcα
102 τὸν θεῖον ὅρκον ἐπὶ τῷ πρωcτίμῳ καὶ πίθωμαι πᾶcι τοῖc
103 ἐγγεγραμμένοιc ὡc πρόκ(ειται) καὶ ὑπογράψαc ἀπέλυcα. † (3d hand) †
Αὐρ(ήλιοc)
104 Μουcῆc Ψαίου cυντελεcτὴc ἀπὸ τῆc α`ὐ´τῆc κώμηc Ἀφροδίτηc
105 εὑρεθεὶc ἐν Ἀντινόου μαρτυρῶ τῇ ὁμολογίᾳ{ν} ἤτοι διαλύcει
106 ἀκούcαc παρὰ τοῦ θεμένου. (4th hand) † Ἑρμαῶc Βόττου ἀπὸ τῆc αὐτῆc
107 κώμηc Ἀφροδίτηc εὑρεθεὶc ἐν Ἀντινόου μαρτυρῶ τῇ
108 διαλυτικῇ ὁμολογίᾳ ἀκούcαc παρὰ τοῦ θεμένου. † (5th hand) † Αὐρήλιοc
109 Cενούθηc Ἀπολλῶτοc ἀπὸ τῆc αὐτῆc κώμηc Ἀφροδίτηc εὑρεθεὶc
110 ἐν Ἀντινόου μαρτυρῶ τῇ διαλυτικῇ ὁμολογίᾳ ἀκούcαc παρὰ τοῦ θεμένου. †

92. ϋποθεμενοc pap. 95. ϋποθηκηc pap. 97. ϋμων ταυθ` pap. 98. Νικαντίνοοc *verschliffen* at the end 99. ϊcιδωρου pap. 100. read ἐcχηκώc ε^{c}χη- corr. from εχε- 101. read εἴκοcι and ὤμοcα 102. ὅρκον corr. from ὅρκων read προcτίμῳ and πείθομαι 103. ὡc corr. from ὅc ϋπογραψαc pap. ἀπέλυcα corr. from ἀπάλαcα 104. ψαϊου pap. Ἀφροδίτηc *verschliffen* at the end 105. iota of εὑρεθείc rewritten

111 (6th hand) † Αὐρήλιοϲ ᾿Απολλῶϲ Βηϲ̣ί̣ου ἀπὸ τῆϲ αὐτῆϲ κώμηϲ ᾿Αφρ[ο]δίτηϲ εὑρ[εθεὶ]ϲ̣

112 ἐν ᾿Αντιν̣όου μ[αρτυ]ρ[ῶ τῇ δ]ιαλ̣[υτ]ι̣κ̣ῇ ὁμο̣λ̣ο̣γί[α̣ ἀκού]ϲαϲ παρὰ τοῦ θεμ̣έ̣[νου].

113 (7th hand) † Φ[..] [..] [...] τα̣.. ου κ̣[ ]ηθ[....]. τ[..]....λ[....]δ..[.....] ἀ̣κο̣ύ̣[ϲ]α̣ϲ̣ π̣αρὰ τοῦ θεμ̣έ[νου].

114-116 illegible traces of three more lines

Commentary

Address (1a-5)

1a-1: Αὐρήλιος Νικαντίνοος Ἰσιδώρου συντελεστὴς ἀπὸ κώμης Ἀφροδίτης] | διάγων ἐνταῦθα ἐπὶ τῆς Ἀντινοέων καλλιπόλεως

1a. Αὐρήλιος Νικαντίνοος Ἰσιδώρου: this man is not known from other texts, nor is his father. Note that his name, Νικαντίνοος, suggests that the connection of his family with Antinoopolis is of long standing–maybe an ancestor won a victory in the games that were held there. On the earlier evidence for games in Antinoopolis, see W. Decker, "Bemerkungen zum Agon für Antinoos in Antinoupolis (Antinoeia)," *Köln. Beitr. z. Sportwiss.* 2 (1974): 38-56. These particular games were discontinued in late antiquity because of their pagan origin, but other games, mainly chariot races, were held in their stead. For an illustrated papyrus from late antique Antinoopolis showing charioteers, see E.G. Turner, "The Charioteers from Antinoe," *JHS* 93 (1973): 192-95.

The use of the expression διάγων ἐνταῦθα, "residing here," in the next line suggests a more permanent presence in Antinoopolis on Nicantinous' part than just for the sake of the dispute. This expression is lacking in the case of Apollos. It denotes an extended stay in another city just short of a permanent change of residence; for the meaning, see especially H. Braunert, *Die Binnenwanderung. Studien zur Sozialgeschichte Ägyptens in der Ptolemäer- und Kaiserzeit* (Bonn, 1964) 304. Note that the witnesses only happen to be conveniently present in Antinoopolis at the time of the dispute, but do not reside there, as the use of εὑρεθείς in their subscriptions shows (see the note on line 105). Business trips from the villages of Upper Egypt to Antinoopolis seem to have been frequent in late antiquity.

Αὐρήλιος before the name is the standard prefix used for ordinary civilians in late antique Egypt and elsewhere. It ultimately goes back to the universal grant of Roman citizenship by Caracalla in A.D.

212. It is used in opposition to Φλάουιος, which is the prefix used for officials and their families. On the finer distinctions of this practice, see J.G. Keenan, "The Names Flavius and Aurelius as Status Designations in Later Roman Egypt," *ZPE* 11 (1973): 33-63 and 13 (1974): 283-304 as well as the addendum "An Afterthought on the Names Flavius and Aurelius," *ZPE* 53 (1983): 245-50. If neither of the two prefixes is used we are sometimes dealing with members of the clergy or monks, but exceptions to this "rule" abound. See the notes on lines 4 and 106.

συντελεστής: "collective taxpayer." This title indicates that Nicantinous was one of the leading inhabitants of Aphrodito, who were collectively held responsible for the collection of taxes in their town, mainly because of their wealth. On this class of people, see the discussion in J. Gascou, "Les grands domaines, la cité et l'état en Égypte byzantine," *T&M* 9 (1985): 49-52, where specific references to Aphrodito can be found as well as to some of the individuals in the present text. The collection of taxes in Aphrodito was a matter for local inhabitants only, because the village dealt with the government directly (on this *autopragia* see our introduction, section 3).

The use of a title like συντελεστής in personal descriptions, as well as the almost universal use of Αὐρήλιος and Φλάουιος, points to an important aspect of late antique society in general: its preoccupation with rank and status. This does not in itself constitute a deviation from earlier practices, but the higher visibility of status through the persistent use of titles may well have reflected an increase of status awareness. We do not want to suggest that status in late antiquity was a verbal construct. It is clear, however, that in our text status designations appear only in the "code words" used by the scribe, which are notably copied by the witnesses.

ἀπὸ κώμης Ἀφροδίτης: in sixth-century documents Aphrodito is still called Aphrodite. Only after the Arab conquest does the spelling usually end in -ώ. The rich data on the village of Aphrodito are collected in A. Calderini, *Dizionario dei nomi geografici dell'Egitto greco-romano* 1.2 (Madrid, 1966) 302-414; additional information can be found in S. Daris, *Dizionario dei nomi geografici dell'Egitto greco-romano, Supplemento* 1 (Milano, 1988) 72. For an attempt at synthesis, announced by J.G. Keenan, see "The Aphrodito Papyri and Village Life in Byzantine Egypt," *BSAC* 26 (1984): 51-63. For a general overview, see our introduction, section 3.

1. ἐπὶ τῆc 'Αντινοέων καλλιπόλεωc: "in the fair city of the Antinoites." For texts in which the various names of the city occur and for more general information, see A. Calderini, op. cit. (note to line 1a) 69-114, and the additional material in S. Daris, op. cit. (note to line 1a) 39. As we mentioned already at the end of section 2 in our introduction, Antinoopolis was the capital of the province of the Lower Thebais and the seat of its judicial and administrative system. That is the reason why the present settlement was drawn up there; see the note on line 9.

Our text provides the earliest evidence for the use of the title καλλίπολιc for Antinoopolis. The use of this word is not limited to Antinoopolis. Other cities in Egypt called καλλίπολιc known to us are Hermopolis (see *P.Stras.* VI 578 of A.D. 505) and Panopolis (see *P.Coll. Youtie* II 92 of 569; the document was drawn up in Antinoopolis); note also Gaza (see *P.Ness.* III 26 of 570) in Palestine. We do not know how cities (apparently of some rank and status) acquired the title, but its use parallels the tendency in late antiquity to make rank and status visible through titles and the like, a phenomenon briefly discussed in the note on the previous line. Cities in the Roman empire indulged in this use of titles already at a much earlier date, as documented by the classic article of L. Robert, "La titulature de Nicée et de Nicomédie: la gloire et la haine," *HSCP* 81 (1977): 1-39. For Egypt, see the collection of data in O. Hornickel, *Ehren- und Rangprädikate in den Papyrusurkunden. Ein Beitrag zum römischen und byzantinischen Titelwesen* (Giessen, 1930) 34-36. It is safe to assume that Antinoopolis had retained its glory in the later Roman period and that its monuments earned it the title καλλίπολιc. Some of these documents were in fact still visible when the French expedition surveyed Egypt under Napoleon; see the relevant plates in the *Description de l'Égypte.*

1-3: Α̣ὐρηλίο̣[ιc] Φ[οιβά]μμ̣[ωνι] | Τριαδέλφου καὶ αὐτῷ cυντελεcτῇ καὶ τῇ τούτου γαμετῇ 'Αναcταcίᾳ τῇ καὶ | Τεκρομπίᾳ θυγατρὶ Μεγάλου ὁρμωμένοιc ἀπὸ τῆc αὐτῆc κώμηc 'Αφροδίτηc

1. Α̣ὐ̣ρ̣η̣λ̣ί̣ο̣[ιc]: the plural is used because both Aurelius Nicantinous and Aurelia Anastasia are referred to.

1-2. Φ̣[οιβά]μ̣μ̣[ωνι] Τριαδέλφου: this man is known from A.D. 526-72 from a number of other texts, which show him to be an enterprising businessman. See J.G. Keenan, "Aurelius Phoibammon, Son of Triadelphus: A Byzantine Egyptian Land Entrepreneur," *BASP* 17 (1980): 145-54. The present text adds interesting details to the sketch given by Keenan. In this case Phoebammon acquires a piece of property, not from a debtor of his own, but from the relatives of a debtor of someone else, and not by default on the part of the debtor, but by ordinary purchase of the property involved.

2. καὶ τῇ τούτου γαμετῇ: τούτου stands for αὐτοῦ (found in line 8) as often in documents of the later Roman period.

2-3. Ἀναcταcίᾳ τῇ καὶ Τεκρομπίᾳ: Anastasia appears only in this text. She is the wife of Phoebammon, son of Triadelphus, and the niece of Apollos, the father of Dioscorus, the notary and poet. She provides the only direct link between the two families and their papers that have come down to us. This text cancels Keenan's speculation that Phoebammon "had little or no family, possibly therefore only his own mouth to feed" in discussing his social status and his advancement to the higher strata of the society of late antique Aphrodito (op. cit. [note to lines 1-2] 154 and footnote 36). See also our introduction, section 6 for the other family members of Nicantinous mentioned in line 14.

3. θυγατρὶ Μεγάλου: the father of Anastasia probably also occurs in *P.Cair.Masp.* III 67283 III 7 as the father of one Dioscorus, a landowner from Aphrodito. If this identification is correct, we are dealing with another case of papponymy in the same family and in the same generation, because the grandfather of this Dioscorus is the same as that of the notary and poet Dioscorus, i.e., Dioscorus the son of Psimanobet (see the family tree on p. 131).

ὁρμωμένοιc: "originating." On the use of this term to indicate the origin of those who are not currently in their home town, see **#23**, 7 n. (bold numbers refer to the list of settlements on pp. 121-7).

4-5: διὰ coῦ Ἀπολλῶτοc Διοσκόρου πρωτοκωμήτου τῆc εἰρημένηc κώμηc θείου σου |[5]| [τ]ῆ[c προγ]εγραμμένηc Ἀναcταcίαc πρὸc μητρὸc χαίρ(ειν)

4. διὰ coῦ Ἀπολλῶτοc Διοcκόρου: Apollos is the grandson of a certain Psimanobet and father of Dioscorus, the notary and poet (see section 4 of our introduction and the family tree on p. 131).

The absence of Αὐρηλίου before Apollos' name should not disturb us. Presumably the *gentilicium* is subsumed under Αὐρηλίο[ιc] in line 1. One might also argue that the scribe simply forgot to insert it here, as the second witness apparently does in line 106, but that is less likely on the part of a meticulous and experienced scribe like ours. It is reading too much into the absence of the *gentilicium* to suppose that Apollos had already become a monk by the date of the present document, and that the scribe deliberately left it out. On this practice in the case of members of the clergy and monks, see the note on line 1a. We do not have to change the date of the document from ca. A.D. 537 to after 538, when Apollos became a monk. See below the discussion on πρωτοκωμήτηc and the introduction, section 5.

In the present document Apollos acts as a representative of his niece and her husband. The latter capacity is stressed again in line 19. On representatives in Graeco-Egyptian law, see the classic statement of L. Wenger, *Die Stellvertretung im Rechte der Papyri* (Leipzig, 1906), who deals mainly with the earlier period. Below in line 64 two kinds of representatives are distinguished, the one with, the other without (written) authorization from the person or persons represented. Presumably Apollos did not need any written authorization to act on behalf of his niece and her husband. No such written authorization is referred to.

πρωτοκωμήτου: "village chief." The term πρωτοκωμήτηc in this period is not used in a general sense of "chief villager (among many)," but in the meaning "head of a village." See the detailed discussion by A. Steinwenter, *Studien zu den koptischen Rechtsurkunden* (Leipzig, 1920) 38-41 and the brief references in G. Rouillard, *L'administration civile de l'Égypte byzantine* (2d ed. Paris, 1928) 68ff. and J. Gascou, op. cit. (note to line 1a): 50-52. Apollos is first called a πρωτοκωμήτηc in A.D. 514 and he seems to have functioned as such throughout most of his life. This title is given to him for the last time when he had already become a monk; see L.S.B. MacCoull, "More Missing Pieces of the Dioscorus Archive," *Actes du IVe Congrès Copte*, Vol. 2 (Louvain-la-Neuve, 1992): 104-6; the Coptic text published there falls between 537/8 and 546/7. His sons Senuthes and Dioscorus later take over their father's position.

εἰρημένηϲ: we have detected no substantial difference between this and related terms used to refer to something or someone mentioned before in the text. Other terms are ὁ αὐτόϲ, ὁ προγεγραμμένοϲ and ὁ προλεχθείϲ, and these are used in a seemingly haphazard way throughout the document.

Agreement proper (6-98)

(i) *General statement of agreement by Nicantinous* (5-6)

5-6: ὁμολογῶ ὑμῖν | [τὰ ἑξῆϲ ὑποτ]εταγμ̣έ̣να

5-6. ὁμολογῶ ὑμῖν [τὰ ἑξῆϲ ὑποτ]εταγμ̣έ̣να: "I acknowledge to you the following." Instead of construing the text with a simple ὁμολογῶ followed by infinitives, Nicantinous first narrates in a more or less detailed fashion the actions undertaken by him and the others (lines 6-28). Later on the text is indeed construed with ὁμολογῶ followed by a set of infinitives (lines 28-76 with ὁμολογῶ occurring only in line 31; see the outline given in our introduction, section 7). A similar way of presenting the material is followed also in other texts giving a rather substantial part of the history of the case at hand, such as *P.Flor.* III 323, 2 (A.D. 525); **#24**, 5 (580/581); **#25**, 16 (583); and **#31**, 5 (6th cent. A.D.). In rhetorical terms we are dealing here with the *narratio* part of the text.

(ii) *Background of the case* (6-28)

(a) *Facts leading up to the present document* (6-17)

6-9: ἐγὼ ὁ προγεγραμμένοϲ Νικαντίνοοϲ ϲυντελεϲτὴϲ | διάλ[υ]ϲι̣[ν ϲ]υ̣νεθέμην καθ' [ὑμῶν τῶν] προγεγραμμένων Φοιβάμ̣μ̣ωνοϲ κα̣ὶ̣ | Ἀναϲταϲίαϲ τῆϲ αὐτῆϲ γαμετῆϲ διὰ ϲοῦ τοῦ προλεχθέντος Ἀπολλῶτος | πρωτοκομήτου (read: πρωτοκωμήτου) ἐν τῷ κατὰ χώραν πολιτικῷ δικαστηρίῳ

7. διά̣λ[υ]ϲ̣ι[ν ϲ]υ̣ν̣εθέμην καθ' [ὑμῶν τῶν] προγεγραμμένων: "I made a settlement with regard to you, the aforementioned." The composite verb ϲυντίθημι is a variation of the simplex τίθημι which is otherwise used in active and middle forms in this part of the text of a διάλυϲιϲ (**#11**, 11, 20 and passim; **#23**, 57; **#35**, 27; cf. also line 91 of our text as well as the formula used by the witnesses: ἀκούϲαϲ παρὰ τοῦ θεμένου). Verbs, such as ποιοῦμαι and ἔρχομαι (in the form ἐλήλυθα as in line 30) εἰϲ, are also found. In a slightly different context ϲυντίθεμαι is found once in a signature to a διάλυϲιϲ in **#20**, 300-1: ϲυθθεέμην τ̣[αύτην] τ̣ὴ̣ν̣ τιάλ̣υ̣ϲ̣ιν (read ϲυνεθέμην ταύτην τὴν διάλυϲιν).

It is hard to see what the scribe intended with the use of the preposition κατά + genitive, which otherwise means "against" in this text. It seems most likely that this is just another instance of the post-classical use of a preposition which is more frequently encountered in late antique documents. It should be understood as having a function equal to πρόϲ or περί + genitive. For other cases, see, e.g., *P.Leid.Inst.* 13, 38 with the note.

9. πρωτοκομήτου: this is the only time the scribe does not correct himself in writing this word. The other times this word occurs in this text (lines 4, 18, 29 and 35) he is careful enough to correct it.

ἐν τῷ κατὰ χώραν πολιτικῷ δικαστηρίῳ: "in the local civil courthouse." The expression κατὰ χώραν is here equivalent to ἐπιχωρίῳ, which we find in line 63 (see the note to lines 63-64). In papyri the only other instance of a πολιτικὸν δικαϲτήριον is *BGU* XII 2173, 2 (of A.D. 498), which also refers to Antinoopolis, as we shall see in a moment. Courts are mentioned more than once in our text (line 63 [*bis*]) as part of a legal formula, but it is only here that the descriptive adjective πολιτικόν is added. We may therefore be dealing with a specific courthouse in Antinoopolis, known as the πολιτικὸν δικαϲτήριον, where the document was drawn up. Document **#41** refers to the actual place where the document was drawn up in three different ways: line 5 is still rather vague (ἐπ' ἀγορᾶϲ), lines 45-46 are more specific (ἐν δημοϲίῳ τόπῳ), but only line 95 identifies the office (ἐν δημοϲίῳ ἀρχείῳ).

The point here no doubt is that Nicantinous and Apollos had come to an agreement in the very building in Antinoopolis where the πολιτικὸν δικαϲτήριον resided and where civil lawsuits were heard. They presumably intended to take the matter to court, but agreed after some discussion not to make use of the very complicated and costly court procedures, as appears from the statement in line 20. On the significance of this detail for our view of the civil courts in late antique Egypt, see our introduction, section 10.

In the *Codex Justinianus* the adjective πολιτικόϲ is frequently employed with the words δικαϲτήριον, δίκη and νόμοϲ, to distinguish courts dealing with secular matters from those dealing with ecclesiastical matters (ἐκκληϲιαϲτικόϲ). Clergy could appeal to secular courts, if they were disappointed by a verdict from an ecclesiastical court, dominated, as these were, by church hierarchy and by the bishop in particular (see *Cod. Just.* I 4, 29, 8 and 11 and I 3, 44, 1). The use of the adjective πολιτικόϲ serves as a means to distinguish the *civil* from the ecclesiastical as well as the *civil* from the military; the latter usage is attested in *P.Cair.Masp.* III 67282, 6 (see the editor's note).

The editor of *BGU* XII 2173 mistranslates the expression πολιτικὸν δικαϲτήριον in his text as "städtisches Gericht." In fact a correct reading of the phrase in which it occurs shows that the civil courthouse in Antinoopolis is meant. The text begins by recounting how someone from Hermopolis deposited a complaint against certain people ἐν τῷ προϲφόρῳ πολιτικῷ δικαϲτηρίῳ, which the editor translates as "beim zuständigen städtischen Gericht." The adjective πρόϲφοροϲ in the meaning "zuständig" is unparalleled in papyri. It once occurs in a legal context with δικασταί (*Cod. Just.* VII 51, 5, 1; cf. also *Novellae* LXXX 6 with ἄρχοντεϲ), but with the expected dative for the matter in which the δικασταί are competent. In *BGU* XII 2173 the πολιτικὸν δικαϲτήριον is already specific enough; adding πρόϲφορον would be redundant. We should therefore read ἐν τῷ πρὸϲ φόρῳ πολιτικῷ δικαϲτηρίῳ and translate "in the civil courthouse at the *forum*." The latter is official jargon for the judicial center of the province. Since the text comes from Hermopolis, which was part of the Lower Thebais, the scribe of the text must be referring to the judicial center of the Lower Thebais, i.e., Antinoopolis. This is also confirmed by the occurrences of the expression φόρου Θηβαίδοϲ in the same text. It may well be that the civil courthouse was literally situated in the central market place in Antinoopolis.

9-10: περὶ τοῦ χρέουϲ |[10]| ὡ̣ϲανεὶ καταβληθέντοϲ παρ' ἐμοῦ τὸ τηνικαῦτα

10. ὡ̣ϲανεὶ καταβληθέντοϲ παρ' ἐμοῦ: instead of ὡ̣ϲανεί the first editor of this part of the text read Π̣τ̣ανει, which he took as a dative of the person to whom Nicantinous paid the debt. From the photo ὡ̣ϲανεί seems much better and removes the awkward intruder Ptanis. Nicantinous paid the debt to the creditor, Iosephius, as one would expect.

The exact meaning of ὡ̣ϲανεί is, however, not very clear at first sight. Properly speaking ὡ̣ϲανεί (sometimes written by editors as one word, sometimes as three words) means "as it were," and syntactically it is connected with the following participle καταβληθέντοϲ. The participle is then qualified by ὡϲανεί either as a metaphor (cf. the modern Greek σαν) or as something that does not necessarily correspond to reality. Since καταβάλλω is an ordinary verb meaning "to pay," we cannot regard ὡϲανεί as an explicit reference to the original metaphor behind the verb ("to cast down"). It seems therefore that Nicantinous somehow wants to stress that there is more than an ordinary payment involved here. But what does he mean by saying that he has acted "as if" he had paid the debt? In our opinion, taking ὡϲανεί to mean that Nicantinous has "sort of" paid the debt, but that no actual payment took place, can be hardly justified. If he intends to convey that he has not really paid the debt yet, it is difficult to see why Apollos agrees to the settlement in the first place. Moreover, Nicantinous is explicitly referring to the actual payment of the debt later on in the text (lines 23 and 43). Because of the complex use of ὡϲανεί, we should seek a solution in light of the other known instances of this word in the papyri.

Papyri in which ὡϲανεί (=ὡϲ ἂν εἰ) occurs are not confined to the later Roman period. The earlier texts are: *P.Cair.Zen.* I 59093, 18 (257 B.C.); *P.Tor.Amen.* 8, 83 (116 B.C.); *BGU* VIII 1816, 11 (60/59 B.C.); *SB* XIV 12138, 11 (1st cent. A.D.); and *P.Oxy.* XLI 2982, 19 (2d/3d cent. A.D.). The later texts are: *SB* III 7033, 60 (481); *P.Hamb.* I 23, 36 (569); **#23**, 12 (6th cent. A.D.); **#37** (p. 206) 36 (6th or 7th cent. A.D.); and *Stud.Pal.* XX 243, 27 (7th cent. A.D.). The text of *P.Oslo* III 83, 14 (3d cent. A.D.) is too fragmentary. In three of these texts ὡϲανεί is construed with a finite verb and in seven with a participle, the present text included. In some of the texts of the later period ὡϲανεί unexpectedly takes on a meaning more akin to Latin *qua* than *quasi*. Except for *Stud.Pal.* XX 243, 27 and the fragmentary

#37 (p. 206) 36, none of the later examples can be rendered satisfactorily by "as if." English "as," "since" or "considering that" seem much better. The first editor of *SB* III 7033, 60 translates ὡcανεί by "ostensibly," which also seems an apt translation in *P.Hamb.* I 23, 36 (not "as if" in contempt of the law, but "ostensibly" so). In **#23**, 12, the point is not, as the editors have it, that one of the siblings was treated differently "as if" he were an adult, but "because" he was an adult at the time the others were not. Thus in our text a rendering "now that the debt has *indeed* been paid by me" seems to be the most appropriate.

ὡc ἄν with a causal function is encountered in earlier periods in literature. In one of the recently published epigrams of Posidippus, the dead Cretan Menoetius, son of Philarchus, discourages all those passing by his tomb from having a discussion with him. Menoetius is a man of few words because he is a foreigner (ὀλιγορρήμων ὡc ἂν ἐπὶ ξενίηc); for the text, see M. Gronewald, "Der neue Poseidippos und Kallimachos Epigramm 35," *ZPE* 99 (1993): 28.

τὸ τηνικαῦτα: "now." This adverb, with or without the article, is not infrequent in late papyri. A close parallel for the present text is **#20**, 86-87: κατέβαλλεν ἐπ' αὐτοὺc τὸ τηνικαῦτα κατὰ τὸν τῆc πράcεωc καιρὸν κ.τ.λ., and also Frag. 1, 324-325: καταβεβλῆ[cθα]ι ἐκ πλήρουc ἐπ' αὐτὸν τὸ τηνικαῦτα.

10-12: ὑπὲρ λυτρώcεωc | [ὑ]π[ο]θήκηc γεγενημένηc παρὰ τῶν αὐτοῦ γονέων εἰc ὄνομα Ἰωcηφίου | [υἱοῦ ὑπὲ]ρ τοῦ κτήματοc ὑποτεθέντοc αὐτῷ παρὰ τῶν ἐμῶν γονέων

10-11. ὑπὲρ λυτρώcεωc [ὑ]π[ο]θήκηc: "for the redemption of a deed of security." For this expression, which refers to the actual delivery of the ὑποθήκη document, see *P.Köln* III 156, 4-5: ἄχρι τῆc το[ῦ χ]ρέουc ἀποδόcεω[c] μετὰ τῆc [παραμ]υθείαc καὶ λυτρώcεωc ταύτηc μου τῆc ὑποθήκηc. This is repeated in line 23 of our document; cf. also line 44.

λυτρόω, λύτρον and λύτρωcιc are the regular technical terms used already in Ptolemaic papyri to denote the redemption of a pledge. With the advent of Christianity λυτρόω and its cognates became the main terms to denote redemption from sin, and Christ is often described as the λυτρωτήc (see the relevant entries in Lampe, *A Patristic Greek Lexicon*). It is unlikely that the use of the word in our text has anything to do with knowledge of Christian doctrine as such, but in a religious sense λύτρωϲιϲ does occur in at least one documentary papyrus: *P.Köln* III 157, 10.

11. γεγενημένηϲ παρὰ τῶν αὐτοῦ γονέων: the reference is presumably to Iosephius' parents (αὐτοῦ meaning "his"), who are mentioned later on in the sentence. We have thought of reading αὑτοῦ instead of αὐτοῦ and taking it as the equivalent of ἐμαυτοῦ, "my own." Evidence for this usage in papyri is extremely rare even in the early Ptolemaic period; see E. Mayser, *Grammatik der griechischen Papyri aus der Ptolemäerzeit* 1.2 (Berlin, 1938) 64. The problem is compounded by the fact that no aspiration was used to distinguish the reflexive from the possessive pronouns which otherwise have the same form. However, aspiration in general seems to make no difference in the late period even in literature; see L. Koenen & C. Römer, *Der Kölner Mani-Kodex. Über das Werden seines Leibes. Kritische Edition* (Opladen, 1988) xxv-xxvi. If we were to understand αὑτοῦ in the sense of ἐμαυτοῦ, Nicantinous would in that case be referring to his own parents. However, he refers to his parents quite explicitly in the rest of the sentence where he mentions that they put the κτῆμα up as security, so that people other than his own parents must be meant here.

It is remarkable that the prepositional phrase παρά + genitive in the parallel expressions [ὑ]π̣[ο]θήκηϲ γεγενημένηϲ παρὰ τῶν αὐτοῦ γονέων and ὑποτεθέντοϲ αὐτῷ παρὰ τῶν ἐμῶν γονέων is used for both the creditors and the debtors. The first expression refers to the document of security that was drawn up in Iosephius' name on the initiative of his (i.e., Iosephius') parents as the creditors to the loan agreement, not *by* them, because that would put them in the position of debtors. The scribe could have used a dative after γεγενημένηϲ here, as he did in line 16, rather than a prepositional phrase. "By" is, however, the correct translation of παρά in the next line; it is the security put up *by* Nicantinous' parents. Similar cases are *P.Michael.* 45, 11, *P.Stras.* IV 248, 5 and V 398, 7-8. The awkward word order of the first expression (γεγενημένηϲ . . . εἰϲ ὄνομα . . .) and the fact that the parents of Iosephius were responsible for having the original document drawn up in the name of their son rather than in their own name may have led the scribe to use the preposition παρά + genitive for the creditors.

εἰϲ ὄνομα 'Ιωϲηφίου: "in favor of Iosephius." The use of the expression εἰϲ ὄνομα means that Iosephius is the beneficiary of the security or, in other words, the creditor. See for a parallel *P.Panop*. 23, 8 of A.D. 314 or after. The parents no doubt came up with the money themselves, but they had the document drawn up in their son's name to provide him with some sort of financial security later on in his life. As it turns out this was indeed an intelligent arrangement, because the present dispute arose after the death of the original debtors, presumably after at least a couple of years. Iosephius now collects in person the debt owed to him by the heir of the original debtors without the assistance of his parents, who may well have died in the meantime.

Iosephius has a very common name and therefore cannot be identified with any known individual from Aphrodito. The text does not indicate where Iosephius comes from. Later on it refers to Iosephius as "the aforementioned" *vel sim.* This leads us to suspect that the identity of Iosephius is not really important in this text and probably that there was no patronymic in the lacuna at the beginning of the next line. The space is too short and it may suffice to read Ἰωϲηφίου [υἱοῦ there.

12. ὑπέ]ρ: "concerning, on behalf." A good parallel of this preposition in combination with ὑποθήκη is provided by *P.Michael.* 45, 7-8.

κτήματοϲ: "estate." In texts of the later Roman period this word commonly refers to a vineyard as opposed to γεώργιον, which refers to an ordinary plot of land. See M. Schnebel, *Die Landwirtschaft im hellenistischen Ägypten* (Munich, 1925) 242, note 5. The location of the κτῆμα is revealed only in lines 46-48.

13-17: κ̣[αὶ διαπ]ραθέντοϲ ὑμῖν τοῖϲ προγεγραμμένοιϲ Φοιβάμμ̇ωνι καὶ | Ἀναϲταϲίᾳ τῇ αὐτοῦ γαμετῇ παρὰ τῶν ἐμῶν ἀδελφιτῶν (read: ἀδελφιδῶν) πρὸ ὀλίγου |[15]| χρόνου, φημὶ δὴ Εὐδοξίαϲ καὶ Ἀντωνίαϲ καὶ Κολλούθου ἀκολούθωϲ | τῇ δυνάμει τῶν γεγενημένων ὑμῖν παρ' αὐτῶν πράϲεων τοῦ αὐτοῦ | κ̣τήματοϲ τῶν καὶ τὴν ἰδίαν ἰϲχὺν ἐχουϲῶν

13. διαπ]ραθέντοϲ ὑμῖν τοῖϲ προγεγραμμένοιϲ: "sold to you, the aforementioned." The supplement [μεταπ]ραθέντοϲ of the first editor is awkward, because it implies that two πράϲειϲ (=sales of land) had taken place and that it came into the possession of Phoebammon and his wife Anastasia

only with the second πρᾶϲιϲ. Moreover, the verb μεταπιπράϲκω is not actually found in other papyri; instead, the papyri use μεταπωλέω (see, e.g., the relevant entry in the *WB*). μεταπιπράϲκω is also rare in literature; LSJ lists only two examples. On the contrary, διαπραθέντοϲ avoids the implication of a previous transfer by sale and because the verb διαπιπράϲκω is regularly used in late antique documents (see the listings in *WB* 1 and 4). Literally διαπιπράϲκω means "to transfer property by a deed of sale." For some very close parallels, see *P.Oxy* XVI 1901, Frag. 6, 28-29 (6th cent. A.D.): καὶ τὸ [ἥ]μ̣ιϲυ μέροϲ [τοῦ ἄ]λλου ἡμίϲουϲ μέρ[ουϲ τοῦ αὐτοῦ οἴκου] τοῦ διαπραθέντοϲ μ̣ο̣[ι πα]ρ̣ὰ̣ Ἐπιφ[ανίου] ἀδελφοῦ (note that the construction is the same as in our papyrus), and *P.Laur.* II 26, 5 (7th cent. A.D.): ὑπὲρ τῶν δ̣ι̣α̣π̣ραθ(έν)τ(ων) [μ]ο̣ι̣ ἐ̣δ̣[α]φ̣ῶν̣ διὰ Θεοδοϲίαϲ (cf. the editor's note to line 5).

14. παρὰ τῶν ἐμῶν ἀδελφιτῶν: "by my nieces and nephew." For the interchange of δ and τ as practiced by Egyptian scribes, see T. Gagos & P. van Minnen, "Documenting the Rural Economy of Byzantine Egypt: Three Papyri from Alabastrine," *JRA* 5 (1992): 196, note to lines 18-21. These letters represent the same phoneme in Coptic and could easily cause confusion to the scribes of the late period.

15. Εὐδοξίαϲ καὶ Ἀντωνίαϲ καὶ Κολλούθου: these relatives of Nicantinous are not listed in V.A. Girgis, *Prosopografia e Afroditopolis* (Berlin, 1938). Also, our Εὐδοξία cannot be identified positively with the well-to-do woman from Aphrodito bearing the same name, who is the sister of a *comes*. She occurs in the papyrus published by J. Gascou & L.S.B. MacCoull, "Le cadastre d'Aphroditô," *T&M* 10 (1987): 103-58 lines 122, 146, 161, 201, and 256.

15-16. ἀκολούθωϲ τῇ δυνάμει: "in accordance with the legal force" is another way of saying κατὰ τὴν δύναμιν, which is found in, e.g., **#20**, 166-67. The entire expression qualifies or explains διαπραθέντοϲ, which in turn specifies the governing documentation of the transfer of the property.

16. τῶν γεγενημένων ὑμῖν παρ' αὐτῶν πράϲεων: the use of the plural ("deeds of sale") can be explained by reference to the fact that three persons are involved as sellers of the property. It might well be that all three

of them drew up separate contracts for their share of the property or rather for their share of the rights on the property. Because Nicantinous' nieces and nephew apparently inherited the property from their aunt and uncle, whereas Nicantinous himself inherited his parents' debt, the situation was even further complicated. In a final act, Nicantinous has to clean up the mess left by his parents and also to resolve the problem created by his nephew and nieces. His presence in Antinoopolis undoubtedly kept his siblings out of the matter altogether. See also our introduction, section 6.

17: τὴν ἰδίαν ἰcχὺν ἐχουcῶν: "which are valid on their own." This means that the contracts of sale made by the siblings are independent of the present agreement, which might have altered the validity of those sales if the parties to the conflict had wanted it. To put it in a different way, both parties recognize that the previous sales are not to be rendered invalid by the present agreement. For contemporary parallels, see **#36**, 6, where it is said of a ὁμολογία παραχωρήσεως: ἥτις καὶ τὴν ἰδίαν περιέχει δύναμιν, and **#22**, 49-50. In our document δύναμις and ἰcχύς seem to have about the same meaning.

(ii) *Background of the case* (6-28)

(b) *Mediation leading up to the present agreement* (17-28)

17-20: καὶ πολλῶν εἰρημένων καὶ | κινηθέντων μεταξὺ ἐμοῦ Νικαντινόου καὶ 'Απολλῶτος πρωτοκωμήτου | ἐπὶ τὰ ἐνταῦθα τοῦ καὶ ἀναπληροῦντος τὴν χώραν ὑμῶν τῶν προ|[20]|γεγραμμένων

17-18. πολλῶν εἰρημένων καὶ κινηθέντων: "after many words have been said and many moves have been made." For a later Byzantine parallel to this formula, see A. Steinwenter, "Das byzantinische Dialysis-Formular," *Studi Aldo Albertoni*, Vol. 1 (Padua, 1935): 85 (with the reference to the publication on p. 76). In a notary's handbook of the twelfth century one of the formulas reads: πολλῶν λόγων μέcον ἡμῶν κινηθέντων. This is part of the description of what led to the settlement agreed upon in the document. The parallel also shows that κινηθέντων in the late period should be interpreted more loosely than κινέω in the technical sense of "bringing forward in court, taking legal action against." Compare, e.g., **#30**, 9, where κινέω is used with (unspecified) λόγουϲ.

The whole point of a settlement like ours is that the parties to the dispute solve the matter by choosing the option of mediation, which involves lengthy discussions and negotiations on the rights and obligations of both parties. Compare **#20**, 52-53, where καὶ πολλῶν ἐπὶ τούτοιϲ λεχθέντων καὶ δικαιολογηθέντων refers to private conversations and conversations with legal advisers. See also **#23**, 22; **#25**, 33-34 n. ("gewiss noch aussergerichtlich" is the comment of the editors); **#27**, 18-19 (καὶ πολλῶν λεχθέντων καὶ ἀντιλεχθέντων καὶ δοκιμαcθέντων); **#28**, 11; **#29**, 30-31; **#32** (p. 201) 28 (with κεινηθέντων); **#41**, 29; *P.Lond.* V 1707, 4; *P.Ness.* III 57, 6; and *P.Oxy.* LVI 3872, 8 for similar phrases in documents of the later Roman period.

19. ἐπὶ τὰ ἐνταῦθα: "here," in Antinoopolis. The phrase should be connected with the preceding participles and not with what follows. The only other parallel papyrus we have been able to find for this expression (meaning "here") is *SB* VI 9376, 3. The first editor of the Vatican portion of our text translates the expression as "a questo riguardo" and connects it with what follows, but such a translation does not explain the position of the expression in the sentence.

τοῦ καὶ ἀναπληροῦντοϲ τὴν χώραν ὑμῶν: the insertion of καί gives this phrase away as an afterthought on Ἀπολλῶτοϲ πρωτοκωμήτου and shows that the now akward, intervening expression ἐπὶ τὰ ἐνταῦθα does not belong to this phrase, but to the preceding. The verb ἀναπληρόω is used in this text with τὴν χώραν and τὴν τάξιν (lines 27-28) in the meaning "to take someone else's place," "to act as a substitute" or "to represent." This meaning is not found in the *Novellae* (CXXXVII 6 princ. refers to someone "who takes the place [τὸν τόπον]" of a lay person, i.e., "is" a lay person). The verb πληρόω is used in a similar sense in **#20**, 58, 92 (with τὸ πρόϲωπον), and 214, and in **#36**, 33. For further examples of Greek expressions referring to representation, see E. von Druffel, *Papyrologische Studien zum byzantinischen Urkundenwesen im Anschluss an P. Heidelberg 311* (Munich, 1915) 34-35.

20-22: πρὸ δίκης καὶ πρὸ διαγνωστικῶν ἀγώνων τέλος φίλοι | ἀγαθοὶ μέσοι ἡμῶν γενόμενοι {οἵτινες} διαλαβόντες τὰ τοῦ πράγματος | ἐδικαίωσαν

20. πρὸ δίκης: "before a lawsuit (took place)." The parties to the conflict agreed to settle their dispute through mediation even before they had initiated a lawsuit. *P.Princ.* II 82, 14 of A.D. 481 records a similar case of settlement πρὸ δίκης, but the agreement there is reached after a petition was filed with the proper authorities by one of the disputing parties. See on this particular aspect of the text W. Ensslin, "Ein Prozessvergleich unter Klerikern vom Jahre 481," *RhM* 75 (1926): 428-32. For the importance of this and the following formula for our views on civil jurisdiction in late antique Egypt, see the introduction, section 10.

πρὸ διαγνωστικῶν ἀγώνων: "before cognition trials (took place)." This particular phrase occurs also in *Novellae* CXV 2. The expression refers to preliminary hearings by a court of law (so-called *cognitiones*, to be distinguished from the actual court session, the δίκη, which was mentioned in the preceding formula). These hearings functioned as a sort of preliminary investigation into the case in order to decide whether to proceed with it in a court of law or to abandon the court as not being a viable option and to resort to mediation or some other alternative. The present case did not even reach the stage of preliminary hearings. Other occurrences of the adjective διαγνωστικός in papyri are *P.Lips.* 34, 15 (c. A.D. 375) and *PSI* VII 768, 13 (465). Both these texts concern διαγνωστικὰ ὑπομνήματα, which are the written recommendations of the courts following their preliminary hearings.

τέλος: "at last." On the adverbial use of the word, as here, see especially **#25**, 34: πολλῶν εἰρημένων μεταξὺ αὐτῶν περὶ τούτου τέλος ἔδοξεν, ὥστε κ.τ.λ. and **#20**, 54, where it is used in a similar phrase, as well as **#41**, 29 and *SB* VI 9456, 12. The word τέλος used adverbially is also very common in modern Greek, but the usage is already attested as early as Herodotus, often at the beginning of a clause. See, e.g., Herodotus I 76: μάχης δὲ καρτερῆς γενομένης, τέλος οὐδέτεροι νικήσαντες διέστησαν.

φίλοι ἀγαθοί: these friends are presumably adult male inhabitants of Aphrodito who happen to be in Antinoopolis at the time of the settlement. It is likely that they are mutual friends of both Nicantinous and Apollos, and it is not unlikely that some of them are among the witnesses to the present settlement, who appended their signatures below.

From an examination of the other settlements which we list on pp. 121-7, we can confirm that in the majority of cases mediation was performed by such mutual friends of the parties to the dispute. Occasionally, however, some official whom both parties could trust acted as a more or less impartial judge of the case. See also our introduction, section 9.

21. μέcοι ἡμῶν γενόμενοι: this refers to the μεcῖται, "mediators," who appear again in lines 30, 37 and 74 and, as mentioned in the previous note, may be some of the witnesses at the bottom of the document. The same kind of people are referred to in **#32** (p. 201) 27 as μέcοι εἰρηνικοὶ ἄνδρεc ἀγαθοί. On the role of arbitration and mediation in the later Roman period as it is known through the agreements of settlement and similar documents, see A. Steinwenter, *Das Recht der koptischen Urkunden* (Munich, 1955) 53-56 and J. Modrzejewski, "Private Arbitration in the Law of Greco-Roman Egypt," *JJP* 6 (1952): 239-56, as well as our introduction, section 9.

In our text it is not stated whether the two parties made a preliminary agreement to seek justice through arbitration. This agreement would have been put in writing in a so-called *compromissum* and should have been mentioned in this final act. There are several examples of such preliminary agreements in Greek and Coptic papyri of later date. See the overview in R. Taubenschlag, *The Law of Greco-Roman Egypt in the Light of the Papyri* (2d ed. Warsaw, 1955) 402-3. We would perhaps expect such a document to be more frequent in cases where the authorities had already been involved. In the present case the parties proceed to mediation without further ado.

{οἵτινεc} διαλαβόντεc τὰ τοῦ πράγματοc: "who, by taking up the case." οἵτινεc is redundant; the construction can do without it. Perhaps the scribe regarded the preceding γενόμενοι as the main verb.

22. ἐδικαίωcαν: "they decided." The use of this verb in later Roman papyri seems confined to *PSI* V 481, 11 and VII 768, 19 and *SB* III 7033, 30 and 33. In the last mentioned text we find it in relation to a μεcιτεία, just as in our text. It is interesting to note that some elements of the terminology used in courts (such as the verb δικαιόω) have been adopted as technical terms also for the mediation process. In functional terms both a lawsuit and mediation indeed served the same end in late antique society.

22-28: ἐμὲ τὸν αὐτὸν Νικαντίνοον λαβεῖν παρ' ὑμῶν ὑπὲρ πάϲη[ϲ] | [ἀ]παλλαγῆϲ τοῦ καταβληθέντοϲ παρ' ἐμοῦ χρέουϲ εἰϲ λύτρωϲιν ὑποθήκηϲ | τοῦ προειρημένου κτήματοϲ χρυϲοῦ νομίϲματα ἑπτὰ ἕκαϲτον |[25]| παρὰ κεράτια δύο τῷ χρυϲοχοϊκῷ ϲταθμῷ τῆϲ εἰρημένηϲ κώμηϲ | Ἀφροδίτηϲ καὶ ϲίτου ἀρτάβαϲ εἴκοϲι πενταμέτρῳ τῷ μέτρῳ ϲου | τοῦ αὐτοῦ Φοιβάμμωνοϲ τοῦ τὴν τάξιν ὑμῶν τῶν προγεγραμμένων | ἀ̣ν̣[α]π̣ληροῦντοϲ

23. ὑπὲρ πάϲη[ϲ] [ἀ]παλλαγῆϲ: "for the complete discharge" of the debt owed to Iosephius by Nicantinous as heir to his parents' estate. For a settlement that uses the word ἀπαλλαγή, see **#20**, 211 and 238.

25. χρυϲοῦ νομίϲματα ἑπτὰ ἕκαϲτον παρὰ κεράτια δύο τῷ χρυϲοχοϊκῷ ϲταθμῷ: "seven solidi minus two carats each according to the goldsmiths' standard." The subtraction of two carats per *solidus* according to the goldsmiths' standard is frequent in texts from the Antaeopolite nome. In texts from the Oxyrhynchite nome we encounter a subtraction of two carats per solidus according to the private standard (ἰδιωτικῷ ζυγῷ), but it is more common to find a subtraction of six carats according to the public standard (δημοσίῳ ζυγῷ). This is also what we find in the texts from the Hermopolite nome. It has sometimes been suggested that this deduction in Aphrodito and Oxyrhynchus was either a tax on transactions involving money or a standardized fee for the handling of money payments. See L.C. West & A.C. Johnson, *Currency in Roman and Byzantine Egypt* (Princeton, 1944) 140ff. and in particular 148-49 and 152-53. M.F. Hendy, *Studies in the Byzantine Monetary Economy, c. 300-1450* (Cambridge, 1985) 346-49, has suggested that the fee was intended to recover the discrepancy between the theoretical and the actual weight of the coins.

Recently, K. Maresch, *Nomismata und Nomismatia. Beiträge zur Geldgeschichte Ägyptens im 6. Jahrhundert n.Chr.* (Opladen, 1994) has demonstrated that different systems developed in different parts of Egypt. Whereas the Oxyrhynchite and Hermopolite nomes used a theoretical solidus of 24 carats of which the private standard was four carates short and the public six, the Antaeopolite nome used a theoretical solidus of which the public standard was two carats short, as it is in our text. The public standards in all nomes were the same. Therefore, 18 carats in the Oxyrhynchite and Hermopolite nomes were equal to 22 carats in the Antaeopolite nome.

The "goldsmiths' standard" (χρυcοχοϊκῷ cταθμῷ) as equivalent to the public standard appears to be used exclusively in documents originating from Aphrodito. Our text may give the impression of being an exception in that respect, but in fact it is not. Although the document is drawn up in Antinoopolis, it includes a stipulation about payment of the seven solidi to Nicantinous according to the goldsmiths' standard of Aphrodito. The disputing parties all originate from Aphrodito and are probably using the standard of that village by default. Goldsmiths are the most likely professionals to own a standard for weighing gold solidi. Overall, the evidence from Aphrodito suggests that their standard became the common standard for the entire village and was frequently employed by those outside their profession. See the note to *P.Hamb.* III 233, 11.

Not all papyri attesting the goldmiths' standard are necessarily from Aphrodito. Some papyri from the archive of Dioscorus have been assigned by their editors to Antinoopolis, but there is always room to argue that the money referred to in those cases will actually change hands in Aphrodito and therefore will be measured with the standard of Aphrodito as in our text. Because there is no comprehensive list of papyri that mention the "goldsmiths' standard," we give them here: *P.Cair.Masp.* I 67006, 26-27; 67036, 4; 67040, 3; 67056 IV 7, 8, 9; 67105, 24; 67106, 19; 67107, 17; 67112, 20; 67116, 5, 11; *P.Flor.* III 290, 6; *P.Hamb.* I 68, 34; III 233, 11; *P.Lond.* V 1667, 6; 1669, 5; 1692 A 17, B 17; 1697, 13; 1701, 3 and 10; 1703, 1; *P.Mich.* XIII 664, 16; 665, 45; *P.Michael.* 43, 13; 45, 41; *P.Ross.Georg.* III 34, 4; 35, 2; *P.Vat.Aphrod.* 1, 27; 6, 7; *SB* III 7201, 14; and our text. One should perhaps reject the restoration of the goldsmiths' standard in the Hermopolite text *P.Herm.* 59, 4.

26. cίτου ἀρτάβαc εἴκοcι: we do not know why Nicantinous is to be paid both in cash and in kind. Perhaps Phoebammon and Anastasia simply could not come up with more than seven solidi in cash. Since the transaction takes place in their absence, it is also possible that Apollos did not have more than seven solidi on hand. Be that as it may, twenty artabas of wheat, worth approximately two solidi by the date of this agreement, are the annual food supply for two adults. This raises the question of how this part of the transaction materialized. Did Apollos cart twenty sacks of

wheat to the civil courthouse to satisfy Nicantinous' claim? This is hard to believe. In all likelihood, Apollos only wrote out an "IOU" for the wheat, and then payment could actually take place in Aphrodito (see also the previous note). Nicantinous presumably still owned other land there, and he could use the wheat for tax payments. We cannot exclude the possibility that Apollos, being an influential man, had contacts in Antinoopolis who could provide him with wheat in case he needed some, and that Nicantinous got it from them on the spot. Apollos certainly was not carrying twenty artabas with him on every business trip to Antinoopolis.

πενταμέτρῳ τῷ μέτρῳ cου: "according to your five-measures standard." This measure, which also occurs in line 38, is described here as being the measure owned by Phoebammon. It is probably the same measure as the one mentioned in *P.Michael.* 44, a text that also relates to Phoebammon. It is called τῷ cῷ μέτρῳ there (line 16).

The present text is the only one in which the word πενταμέτρῳ is written out in full. It occurs in abbreviated form in combination with διμάτια in the metrological text *P.Lond.* V 1718. Lines 66-67 of the text (partially resolved) run as follows:

ἡ ἀρτάβη ἔχει διμάτια ε μετρ   ε

ἡ ἀρτάβη ἔχει διμάτια ς μετρ   ς

The editor fails to give the correct expansion (πενταμέτρῳ and ἑξαμέτρῳ respectively) of the abbreviated forms in his introduction to the text. He rightly rejects the possibility of taking ε μετρ and ς μετρ as πεντάμετρα and ἑξάμετρα respectively, because these would be adjectives referring to the capacity of the διμάτια themselves. In that case, there would be a conflicting number of μέτρα (whatever that may be) to the artaba, viz. 5 x 5 = 25 and 6 x 6 = 36 respectively, because the text plainly says that it takes 5 διμάτια ε μετρ or 6 διμάτια ς μετρ to get an artaba. In reality ε μετρ and ς μετρ refer to the different standards used to measure the wheat, and they should therefore be expanded to datives just as in our text. The ἑξάμετρον standard occurs written out in full (ἑξαμέτρῳ) in *P.Cair.Masp.* III 67303, 18 and in one early fourth-century text, *CPR* VI 74, 7, 12 and 14.

There were two different systems used to measure wheat, one decimal, one duodecimal. In the first system the artaba was divided into ten equal parts (μέτρα or μάτια) or five double parts (διμάτια), in the second system the artaba was divided into twelve equal parts or six double parts. The use of πενταμέτρῳ and ἑξαμέτρῳ for the decimal and the duodecimal system respectively shows that the double part (διμάτιον) was the smallest unit of measurement. We do not know for certain what the exact capacity of the artaba according to different systems was, but it seems that the artaba πενταμέτρῳ consisted of 10/3 modii and the artaba ἑξαμέτρῳ of 36/11 modii. The latter was thus slightly smaller than the former. See K. Maresch & P.J. Sijpesteijn, "P.Lond. III 1077 descr.: metrologische Tabellen,"*ZPE* 99 (1993): 59-66.

In *P.Fay.* 90, 14 a μέτρον ἑνδεκάμετρον occurs. This is best explained as a standard according to which it takes eleven parts (μέτρα) to get an artaba. This is exactly in between the decimal and the duodecimal system. It is tempting to equate this measure with the μέτρον 'Αθηναῖον attested in Hermopolis, which seems to have consisted of 11/3 modii and is the largest artaba on record. We should distinguish from all these measures the ἑπτάμετρον standard, which occurs a few times in earlier periods and was used by ἐλαιουργοί to measure the seed called λαχανόcπερμον and the oil they made out of it.

27. τάξιν: here equivalent to χώραν in the meaning "place, position, role" as in line 19 (see the note there).

(iii) *Terms and conditions* (28-81)

28-34: τούτων τοίνυν οὕτω γενομένων καὶ cτερχθέντων καὶ | ἀρεcθέντων ἐμοί τε Νικαντινόῳ̣ καὶ 'Απολλῶτι πρωτοκωμήτῃ̣ |[30]| πρὸc τὴν κρίcιν τῶν μέcων φίλων τούτου ἕνεκα εἰc ταύτην ἐλήλυθα | τὴν ἔγγραφον διαλυτικὴν ὁμολογίαν δι' ἧc ὁμολογῶ ἐγὼ ὁ προγεγραμ|μένοc Νικαντίνοοc ἑκουcίᾳ̣ γνώμῃ̣ καὶ προαιρέcει ἰδίᾳ̣ ἀμετανοήτῳ̣ καὶ | ἀδόλῳ̣ β̣ουλήcει, ὀρθῇ̣ διανοίᾳ̣ δίχα δόλου παντὸc καὶ φόβου καὶ βίαc κ̇αὶ̇ | ἀπάτηc καὶ ἀνάγκηc

28. τούτων τοίνυν οὕτω γενομένων: this wraps up the narrative part (*narratio*) of the case or, in other words, the background of the present agreement (lines 6-28) and serves as a transitional device to the agree-

ment proper. The participles are causal and they anticipate τούτου ἕνεκα in line 30.

cτερχθέντων: "pleased." This strong verb occurs more often, e.g., in **#35**, 21 and especially **#20**, 136, where it is used in a very similar context: τούτων τοίνυν οὕτω δοξάντων καὶ cτερχθέντων.

30. πρὸc τὴν κρίcιν: "in accordance with the judgment." This phrase might go with the preceding genitive absolutes, but in light of the repetition of the phrase in line 37 it should properly be taken with ἐλήλυθα. The document of settlement is of course one of the things the mediators suggested. Note that later on their κρίcιc is explicitly called δικαία (line 37). Again the terminology of court language is used to describe what the mediators are doing (see note to line 22).

τούτου ἕνεκα: the expression summarizes the causal participles in line 28.

31. διαλυτικήν: for parallel texts where this adjective is used, see the list of settlements on pp. 121-7.

32-33. ἑκουcίᾳ γνώμῃ καὶ προαιρέcει ἰδίᾳ ἀμετανοήτῳ καὶ ἀδόλῳ βουλήcει, ὀρθῇ διανοίᾳ δίχα δόλου παντὸc καὶ φόβου καὶ βίαc καὶ ἀπάτηc καὶ ἀνάγκηc: for parallels, see especially **#21**, 3-7; **#23**, 29-30; **#24**, 2-3 and 7-8; **#29**, 59-62 (an even more elaborate formula); **#35**, 7; **#40**, 2-6 (another instance of an even more elaborate formula); **#41**, 49-52; and *P.Cair.Masp.* I 67032, 7-9. A similar expression is also found in *P.Ryl.copt.* 183, a late Coptic διάλυcιc from Hermopolis. More parallels can be found in H. Zilliacus, *Zur Abundanz der spätgriechischen Gebrauchssprache* (Helsinki, 1967) 40-41.

Although there is some repetition of thought, it should be noted that the formula is still meaningful. The text makes Nicantinous explicitly say (1) that he agrees to the present settlement out of his own free will (ἑκουcίᾳ γνώμῃ καὶ προαιρέcει ἰδίᾳ), (2) that he is not going to change his mind (ἀμετανοήτῳ), (3) that he has no intention of cheating the other party (ἀδόλῳ βουλήcει and δίχα δόλου παντὸc), (4) that he knows perfectly well what he is doing (ὀρθῇ διανοίᾳ), and (5) that it is not external pressure on him that makes him draw up this contract (δίχα φόβου καὶ βίαc καὶ ἀπάτηc καὶ ἀνάγκηc). This seeming duplication of words is well entrenched in the history of law and it effectively annuls in advance the possibility of future disputes on any of the grounds mentioned.

The adjective ἀμετανόητος ("irrevocable") is commonly used with a negative connotation and in a religious sense ("unrepentant"), even in the *Novellae* (CXLI praef.). Here, however, it should be understood in a more general, positive, sense. A positive meaning is attested in documentary texts from the Christian period. The earliest reference is *P.Lond.* VI 1913, a contract for the appointment of a deputy dated to A.D. 334, where we find in line 11 ηὐδόκ̣ηcαν . . . ἀμ̣ε̣[ταν]ο̣ή̣τ̣ῳ γ̣ν̣ώμ̣η̣.

(a) *Receipt of payment* (34-40)

34-40: εἰληφέναι μὲν καὶ πεπληρῶcθαι παρ' ὑμῶν τῶν |35| προγεγραμμένων Φοιβάμμωνος καὶ 'Αναcταcίαc διὰ coῦ τοῦ προ|λεχθέντος 'Απολλῶτος πρωτοκωμήτου τῶν δοξάντων δίδοcθαί μοι | πρὸc τὴν δικαίαν κρίcιν τῶν μέcων φίλων, τουτέστιν νομίcματα | ἑπτὰ παρὰ κεράτια δεκατέccαρα καὶ cίτου ἀρτάβαc εἴκοcι πενταμέτρῳ, | πρὸc τῶ (read: τό) ἐμὲ ἀπ' ἐντεῦθεν ἤδη ἀναδοῦναί coι τὴν αὐτὴν ὑποθήκην |40| εἰc ἀκύρωcιν

36. τῶν δοξάντων δίδοcθαί μοι: the participle, which is specified by τουτέστιν νομίcματα ἑπτὰ παρὰ κεράτια δεκατέccαρα καὶ cίτου ἀρτάβαc εἴκοcι πενταμέτρῳ in lines 37-38, should be in the accusative to serve as the direct object of the infinitives εἰληφέναι and πεπληρῶcθαι, as it is correctly written in lines 54 and 73. Here, however, it seems that the use of the verb πληρόω, which is absent in the other two instances, has confused the scribe. πληρόω can be construed with both genitive and accusative, but the message that the scribe is trying to convey here requires a simple accusative.

39. πρὸc τώ: "in order that." πρὸc τό followed by an infinitive is just one of the ways to denote purpose or consequence. See, e.g., B.G. Mandilaras, *The Verb in the Greek Non-literary Papyri* (Athens, 1973) §861 (1). On the almost universal spelling πρὸc τώ in late antique documents, see *P.Michael.* 40, 29 n. It is likely that our scribe thought a dative (πρὸc τῷ) was grammatically correct here.

ἀπ' ἐντεῦθεν ἤδη: a very forceful way of saying that Nicantinous is handing over the deed of security "right now."

40. εἰς ἀκύρωςιν: "for cancellation." Very frequently documents are canceled with strokes of ink, rendering them invalid. To that end the canceled document is transferred from one party to the other, in our case from the original debtor (Nicantinous) to the present owners of the property (Phoebammon and Anastasia, through Apollos). This puts the minds of the latter at rest.

(b) *Renunciation of claims* (40-51)

40-43: μηδένα δὲ λόγον ἔχειν ἢ ἕξειν πρὸς ὑμᾶς καὶ κληρονόμους | ὑμῶν καὶ διαδόχους καὶ διακατόχους, μὴ πρὸς τὸν αὐτὸν Ἀπολλῶν | καὶ τοὺς αὐτοῦ κληρονόμους, οὐκ ἐγώ, οὐ κληρονόμοι μου, οὐ διάδοχοι, | οὐ διακάτοχοι

40-41. καὶ κληρονόμους ὑμῶν καὶ διαδόχους καὶ διακατόχους: "and your heirs and successors and their substitutes by default." If we want to press the exact meaning of the expressions used here and in lines 42-43, we may distinguish between the heirs whose names are mentioned in a testament (κληρονόμοι), the next of kin of those who died intestate (διάδοχοι), and those appointed to be the heirs of those who died intestate and without next of kin (διακάτοχοι). For the distinction, see the very full note at **#23**, 38; see further, R. Taubenschlag, op. cit. (note to line 21) 183. In later Greek law this clear-cut distinction was blurred, and this may be the case in our document. Cf. H. Kreller,"Διάδοχος und κληρονόμος," *Papyri und Altertumswissenschaft* (Munich, 1934) 233ff. and H. Zilliacus, op. cit. (note to lines 32-33) 43-44. The term διακατοχή, which is equivalent to the Latin *bonorum possessio*, is used in the context of intestate inheritance for those who are not next of kin of the deceased. This term is not particularly common and is encountered only in a few Greek legal texts of later date. See, e.g., *Cod. Just.* VI 4, 4, 14a, where the subject is property inherited by freedmen in the absence of legal heirs (κληρονόμοι) or other next of kin (διάδοχοι). On the Latin equivalent, see A. Berger, *Encyclopedic Dictionary of Roman Law* (Philadelphia, 1953) s.v. *bonorum possessio.*

For papyrus parallels, see **#20**, 251-52; **#21**, 14-15; **#23**, 38; **#24**, 8-9, where the editor supplies μὴ [ἄλλον τινά after μὴ διαδόχους, which may have to be changed to μὴ [διακατόχουϲ; **#30**, 17-18; **#31**, 39-40; **#32**, 53-54; **#35**, 16-17, which is more elaborate than our text; and **#41**, 53-54.

42-43. οὐκ ἐγὼ οὐ κληρονόμοι μου οὐ διάδοχοι οὐ διακάτοχοι: as subjects of the preceding infinitives these should all have been in the accusative. However, it seems that the scribe preferred a parenthetic independent sentence which, syntactically, is connected loosely with ὁμολογῶ in line 5 by means of a common subject (ἐγώ).

43-51: μὴ περὶ τοῦ αὐτοῦ χρέουϲ τοῦ καταβληθέντοϲ παρ' ἐμοῦ | τὸ τηνικαῦτα Ἰωϲηφίῳ εἰϲ λύτρωϲιν τοῦ αὐτοῦ κτήματοϲ, μὴ περὶ |[45]| τῆϲ εἰρημένηϲ ὑποθήκηϲ, μὴ περὶ νομῆϲ ἢ δεϲποτείαϲ τοῦ προ|ειρημένου κτήματοϲ τοῦ διακειμένου ἐμ (read: ἐν) πεδιάδι τῆϲ αὐτῆϲ κώμηϲ | Ἀφροδίτηϲ ἐν κλήρῳ καλούμενον (read: καλουμένῳ) Μουνλακον ἐκ νότου τῆϲ ὁδοῦ | τῆϲ βαλλούϲηϲ ἐπὶ τὴν κώμην Τμονεχθη, μὴ περὶ προϲόδων τούτου, | μὴ περὶ οἱουδήποτε πράγματοϲ ἀνήκοντοϲ τῷ αὐτῷ κτήματι δικαίῳ |[50]| ἢ μὴ ἀνήκοντοϲ, μικροῦ ἢ μεγάλου, ἐγγράφου ἢ ἀγράφου, ἀκρίτου ἢ | κεκριμένου τὸ ϲύνολον

45. νομῆϲ ἢ δεϲποτείαϲ: the legal distinction between these two nouns can be rendered in English as follows: νομή is the mere possession (*possessio*), δεϲποτεία the legal ownership (*dominium*) of the property. See R. Taubenschlag, op. cit. (note to line 21) 231.

46. ἐμ πεδιάδι: we find several "plains" in papyri from Aphrodito. The plot described in our document might have been in the plain east of Aphrodito, the ἀπηλιωτικὴ πεδιάϲ (see the list in A. Calderini, op. cit. [note to line 1a] 1.2, 314-23). The majority of the texts seems to suggest that the village Θμονάχθη was located in that plain (see also the note to line 48).

47. ἐν κλήρῳ καλούμενον Μουνλακον: the horizontal bars above the words Μουνλακον and Θμονεχθη in the next line derive from a common practice in documents from late antique Aphrodito. These horizontal bars are used to highlight important geographical details. In late antique texts from Syene we often find such bars written above personal names as

well. In general, these horizontal bars are found frequently, written above important details in the text, such as exact amounts of money or produce, etc.

Μουνλακον is attested in a good number of texts. The spelling varies greatly, but most of the variants start with the Coptic masculine article *p*. See the references in J. Gascou & L.S.B. MacCoull, op. cit. (note to line 15) 138, note on line 81. See especially *P.Michael.* 44, 13 (A.D. 527), where the same Phoebammon as in the present text seems to have a hold on a piece of land that a soldier used as security to obtain a loan from him. In line 12 of that text we no doubt have to read γεώργιον καλού[μενον] rather than the editor's γεωργικ̣ο̣ῦ̣ κλ̣ή̣ρ̣ο̣υ̣ [περί]. The piece of land is called Τ̣μουνλακον in the following line in that text. Because Coptic *mou* (in the Sahidic dialect usually *ma*) *n*, "place of," is a suitable masculine word for a geographical name, we should probably correct the reading to Πμουνλακον in *P.Michael.* 44, 13. Consequently, we must remove the spelling Τμουνλακον from A. Calderini & S. Daris, op. cit. (note to line 1a) and add the Michaelides papyrus to the references for Πμουνλακον. Note that the name in the next line is based on Coptic *moue n*, "island of," which is a feminine word and, therefore, is prefixed by the Coptic feminine article, whereas Πμουνλακον starts with a masculine word and is therefore prefixed by the Coptic masculine article.

48. ἐπὶ τὴν κώμην Τμονεχθη: the name of this village is also spelled Θμοναχθη in other texts. The village is known from several texts of later date, for which, see A. Calderini & S. Daris, op. cit. (note to line 1a) 2, 287; add *P.Mich.* XIII 670, 12. According to *P.Cair.Masp.* III 67329 the same Apollos who acts as a representative in the present document is defending his village's position with regard to some land at Θμοναχθη in A.D. 524/525 (the date according to the *Berichtigungsliste* 4, 15).

49. δικαίῳ: "by legal right." This independent dative expression occurs also in lines 25-26 and in line 51 (δεcποτικῷ̣ δικαίῳ̣).

50. ἢ μὴ ἀνήκοντος: "or which does not belong to it." Strictly speaking this does not make sense coming after ἀνήκοντος, but the phrase also occurs in *SB* III 7033, 63 in a similar context. For a similarly illogical expression in Dutch legalese cf. "onder en boven de wet" ("under and above the law"), which is equivalent to "boven de wet" ("above the law"). In our text there are several antithetical pairs, such as ἀνήκοντοϲ ἢ

μὴ ἀνήκοντος. In addition to those in lines 49-51, see also lines 59, 62 and 89. These "polar" expressions (*polare Ausdrucksweise*) are very common and aim at covering all possible aspects of an issue or object. In Greek, this linguistic feature is already attested in archaic literature. It developed and matured under the influence of rhetoric. For the use of polar expressions in archaic and classical literature with bibliography, see M.L. West, *Hesiod, Works and Days: Prolegomena and Commentary* (Oxford, 1978), note to line 175.

The inclusion of this kind of formula was, however, not wholly without reason. In Roman legal practice, items of dispute settled intentionally but not *disertis verbis* in a *stipulatio Aquiliana* could not be regarded as settled unless a special provision was made in the document to cover those items. This is made clear in a scholion on *Basilica* XI 1, 35 (vol. 1, p. 621 in Heimbach's edition, Vol. B 1, p. 281 in Scheltema's edition), which explains that even after a settlement an item that has not been dealt with expressly can be claimed afterwards: τοῦτο δὲ νόηϲον, κἂν Ἀκουιλιανὴ ὁμολογία γεγένηται, πλὴν εἰ μὴ ἄρα ἰδικῶϲ καὶ τοῖϲ μὴ ἐνθυμηθεῖϲι κατὰ τὸ ϲυνειθιϲμένον ἀπετάξαντο. φύϲιϲ μὲν γὰρ τῇ Ἀκουιλιανῇ ὁμολογίᾳ, μόναϲ ἐκείναϲ καταφέρειν τὰϲ ἀγωγάϲ, περὶ ὧν οἱ τὴν διάλυϲιν πεποιηκότεϲ ἐνεθυμήθηϲαν· ἀπὸ δὲ τῶν ἐξ ἔθουϲ ἐντιθεμένων ταῖϲ Ἀκουιλιαναῖϲ ὁμολογίαιϲ ῥημάτων, δι' ὧν, ὡϲ εἶπον, καὶ τοῖϲ μὴ ἐνθυμηθεῖϲι ἀποτάϲϲονται, ἀναιρεῖται αὐτῷ καὶ ὁ περὶ τῶν μὴ ἐνθυμηθέντων λόγοϲ, ἐπειδὴ πᾶϲα διάλυϲιϲ περὶ τῶν ϲυναρεϲάντων τοῖϲ μέρεϲι γεγενῆϲθαι δοκεῖ. ϲυνήρεϲε δὲ διὰ τῶν ϲυνειθιϲμένων, ὡϲ εἶπον, ῥημάτων, καὶ τοῖϲ μὴ ἐνθυμηθεῖϲιν αὐτοὺϲ ἀποτάξαϲθαι. This is repeated in *Basilica* XI 2, 4 (Vol. 1, p. 670 in Heimbach's edition, Vol. B 1, p. 367 in Scheltema's edition), where the words actually inserted in the documents are given as follows: μὴ περὶ ἑτέρου τινὸϲ τὸ ϲύνολον πράγματοϲ ῥηθέντοϲ ἢ μὴ ἐκφωνηθέντοϲ ἢ μὴ νοηθέντοϲ ἢ ἐνθυμηθέντοϲ ἢ μὴ ἐνθυμηθέντοϲ καταχθέντοϲ ἰδικῶϲ εἰϲ τήνδε τὴν Ἀκουιλιανὴν ὁμολογίαν.

Late Roman papyri relating to settlement of disputes eloquently illustrate the custom of inserting a clause that covers even claims not dealt with at the time of settlement. See, e.g., **#20**, 243-46; **#22**, 30-32; **#23**, 35-37; **#24**, 11; and especially **#21**, 20-24, which contains by far the most elaborate example of this type of clause. A good parallel is provided by the so-called μὴ ἐλαττουμένου μου clause in repayments of loans from the earlier Roman period. This clause is inserted to make sure that other outstanding claims are not annulled by the repayment of a particular loan.

See on this device G. Häge, "Die μὴ ἐλαττουμένου-Klausel in den griechischen Papyri Ägyptens," *Proc. Twelfth Int. Congr. Papyr.* (Toronto, 1970): 195-205.

50-51. ἀκρίτου ἢ κεκριμένου: for a parallel instance in a settlement of a dispute, see **#2**, 13. The same expression is also used in the contract of divorce *P.Lond.* V 1712, 14-15 (from Antinoopolis; A.D. 569).

τὸ cύνολον: here as well as in line 72 this word comes immediately after a long string of negatives introduced by μὴ or μηδένα and means "whatsoever."

(c) *Confirmation of ownership* (51-57)

51-57: ἀλλ' ἔχειν ὑμᾶc δεcποτικῷ δικαίῳ ἐπὶ τὸ | διηνεκὲc τὴν νομὴν καὶ τὴν δεcποτείαν τοῦ προειρημένου κτήματοc | μετὰ παντὸc αὐτοῦ τοῦ δικαίου διὰ τὸ ἐμὲ εἰληφέναι ἐκ πλήρουc | τὰ δόξαντα δίδοcθαί μοι παρ' ὑμῶν διὰ cοῦ τοῦ προλεχθέντοc |[55]| 'Απολλῶτοc, τουτέcτιν νομίcματα ἑπτὰ παρὰ κεράτια δεκατέccαρα | χρυcοχοϊκῷ cταθμῷ τῆc εἰρημένηc κώμηc καὶ cίτου ἀρτάβαc | εἴκοcι πενταμέτρῳ

For commentary on these lines, see especially the notes to lines 34-38.

54. τὰ δόξαντα: here and in line 73 this word is the direct object of εἰληφέναι. However, contrast line 36 and see the note there.

(d) *Settlement proper* (57-76)

57-61: καὶ ἀπηλλάχθαι καὶ διαλελύcθαι πρὸc ὑμᾶc ἐν ἅπαcι | καὶ μηδεμίαν μοι τοῦ λοιποῦ cῴζεcθαι καθ' ὑμῶν οἱανδήποτε ἀγωγὴν | εἰc πρόcωπον ἢ \`καὶ´ εἰc πρᾶγμα ἁρμοcάcηc (read: ἁρμόcαcαν) ἢ καὶ ἁρμόcοι (read: ἁρμόcαι) δυναμένηc (read: δυναμένην) |[60]| ἐκ παντὸc τοῦ προλαβόντοc χρόνου μέχρι τῆc cήμερον καὶ προ|γεγραμμένηc ἡμέραc καὶ εἰc τὸν ἑξῆc ἅπαντα καὶ διηνεκῆ χρόνον

57. ἀπηλλάχθαι καὶ διαλελύcθαι πρὸc ὑμᾶc: for the meaning "to be dismissed as settled" of the first-mentioned verb, see LSJ s.v. ἀπαλλάccω B I 4.

58. τοῦ λοιποῦ: this adverbial expression meaning "from now on" occurs not infrequently in late antique documents and is used again in line 70 in a similar context.

ἀγωγήν: "action," equivalent to Latin *actio*. See the following notes on the various forms of legal action available according to late antique texts. Note the combination ὑποθηκαρία ἀγωγή, which occurs twice in the *Novellae* (IV 2; CXI 1) and once in the *Edictum graecum* (7, 3), and denotes the form of legal action recommended in a case involving security.

59. εἰς πρόσωπον ἢ \`καὶ´ εἰς πρᾶγμα: the same expression also occurs in line 69. This expression ("either personally or with regard to property") occurs in two other settlements: *SB* III 7033, 68 (as corrected in *P.Princ.* II 82) and **#22**, 35-36. It is equivalent to the Latin *in personam vel in rem.* For the Latin cf. A. Berger, op. cit. (note to lines 40-41) s.v. *actiones in personam.* Nicantinous renounces any claim he might have on the other party to the conflict (the *persona*) or on the property involved (the *res*).

In Greek legal texts of the later Roman empire the expression εἰς πρόσωπον has a technical meaning that is irrelevant here: "in the name of, on behalf of, representing." See for this I. Avotins, *On the Greek of the Code of Justinian* (Hildesheim, Zürich, and New York, 1989) 138-39.

ἁρμοσάσης ἢ καὶ ἁρμόσοι δυναμένης: "whether (the action) is fitting or can be made to fit." Since this goes with ἀγωγήν in the preceding line, it should have been in the accusative. This is another instance of a polar expression (see note to line 50). It is used to exclude all possible legal action that might be taken, whether it is directly applicable to the case or can be made to apply; see the parallels from papyri, *CPR* VII 27, 2-3 (with ἀγωγαί) and **#20**, 204-5 (with λόγους), **#23**, 43 (with ἐναγωγή) and **#41**, 49-50 (with δικαιολογία), as well as the parallels from legal texts of later date, such as *Cod. Just.* I 2, 15, 2: τὴν ἐκ ταύτης ἡμῶν τῆς θείας διατάξεως ἁρμόζουσαν ἀγωγὴν κινεῖν κ.τ.λ.

The distinction between the two kinds of action stipulated in this formula originates in Roman law. The ἀγωγὴ ἁρμόζουσα is equivalent to the *actio ex lege*, the statutory action, in which the details of the actual case correspond exactly to the case as described in the law or statute. The ἀγωγὴ ἁρμόσαι δυναμένη corresponds to the *actio utilis*, the analogous or parallel action, whereby the case as described in the law has to be adapted or extended to cover the details of the actual case. An introductory work on this topic is V. Arangio-Ruiz, *Cours de droit romain (les actions)* (Naples, 1935).

The tripartite division of time should probably be classified as a polar expression as well (see above on line 50). The reference to past (ἐκ παντὸς τοῦ προλαβόντος χρόνου), present (μέχρι τῆς σήμερον καὶ προγεγραμμένης ἡμέρας), and future (καὶ εἰς τὸν ἑξῆς ἅπαντα καὶ διηνεκῆ χρόνον) aims at excluding every possibility of legal action. This section stresses the time aspect.

61-64: καὶ | μὴ δύναςθαί μέ ποτε καιρῷ ἢ χρόνῳ ἐγκαλεῖν ὑμῖν καὶ τοῖς ὑμῶν | κληρονόμοις ἐν δικαςτηρίοις καὶ ἐκτὸς δικαςτηρίων ἐπιχωρίῳ | ἢ ὑπερορίῳ μὴ δι' ἐμοῦ, μὴ δι' ἐντολέως, μὴ διὰ παρενθέτου προςώπου

For the stipulations in these and the following lines a close parallel is provided by **#20**, 247ff.

62. καιρῷ ἢ χρόνῳ: the original distinction between these two words seems to be blurred in later Greek. The editors of **#29**, 69 and 75, translate the phrase as: "bei irgendeiner Gelegenheit oder zu irgendeiner Zeit." The editors of *P.Oxy.* I 139, 18-19, translate the phrase as: "at any season or time." These two words indeed overlap in meaning in the later period. In legal documents, such as ours, they are treated almost as synonyms and are used in a way similar to polar expressions (see note to line 50) for the sake of completeness.

63. ἐκτὸς δικαςτηρίων: "out of court." The following ἐπιχωρίῳ ἢ ὑπερορίῳ resumes the preceding ἐν δικαςτηρίοις after a hyperbaton. For close parallels to the phrase ἐν δικαςτηρίοις καὶ ἐκτὸς δικαςτηρίων, see **#41**, 76-77, where we read ἐν δικαςτηρίῳ ἢ ἐκτὸς δικαςτηρίων ἐνορίῳ (the editor prints incorrectly ἐν ὁρίῳ,) ἢ ὑπερορίῳ, an example of the same peculiar, but rhetorically efficient, construction as in our text; **#20**, 248-49; **#21**, 26-27; **#22**, 18; **#23**, 41-42; **#24**, 59-60; **#29**, 70 and 82-83; **#30**, 19-20; **#32**, 51-52; **#35**, 16; and *SB* III 7033, 51-52 and 58-59. In *SB* I 4959, 5 one should supply [δικαςτηρίου] to complement the formula in that text. Cf. also the remarks in *P.Coll.Youtie* II, pp. 600-601.

63-64. ἐν δικαστηρίοις . . . ἐπιχωρίῳ ἢ ὑπερορίῳ: "in courts of law, be they local or elsewhere." The adjective ἐπιχώριος refers to the courts of the χώρα. The correct way to interpret χώρα here is suggested by the very similar expression κατὰ χώραν in line 9, where the local civil court in Antinoopolis is meant, the exact place where the present agreement was reached. The adjective ἐπιχώριος, therefore, should probably be taken to refer to the local court in Antinoopolis in contradistinction to all those elsewhere, rather than to the courts in the Lower Thebais in contradistinction to those outside the Lower Thebais. In the note to **#25**, 59ff. the editors take the latter stance. The adjective ὑπερόριος refers to any court outside Antinoopolis, e.g., the courts in the rest of the Lower Thebais–unless we assume that there were no civil courts in the Lower Thebais outside its capital, Antinoopolis,–the courts in the rest of Egypt, in Alexandria or in Constantinople, etc. For direct parallels to the expression in our text, see also **#20**, 248-49; **#21**, 26; **#29**, 70. The whole judicial system of late antique Egypt is the subject of a lengthy discussion by G. Rouillard, op. cit. (note to line 4) 149-67.

64. μὴ δι' ἐντολέως: on this "authorized representative" in documents from late antique Egypt, see especially *P.Oxy.* XVI 1882, 5 n. and **#29**, 71 n. See also *P.Oxy.* XIX 2244, 64 and *BGU* XII 2173, 1 with the note. For parallels for the phrase μ]ὴ δι' ἐμοῦ ... προσώπου, see **#20**, 250-51; **#21**, 27-28; **#25**, 57-59; **#29**, 70-71 and 83-85; **#30**, 20 (cf. line 36); and **#41**, 77-78.

μὴ διὰ παρενθέτου προσώπου: this "man of straw" is equivalent to Latin *persona interposita*, an intermediary, as opposed to the authorized representative of the previous note. See **#25**, 59, n.

65-67: ἢ θείας φιλοτιμίας ἢ πραγματικοῦ τύπου ἢ ῥεσκρίπτου ἢ θείου | νεύματος ἢ δικανικῆς λεπτολογίας ἢ ἑτέρας οἱασδήποτε αἰτίας | συμβῇ ταύτην ἀτονῆσαι ἢ μέρους (read: μέρος) αὐτῆς

65. θείας φιλοτιμίας: it is difficult to see why "imperial generosity" or "liberality" or "munificence" is mentioned here as a factor that could render the present agreement ineffective. This expression, the first in a string of causal genitives, probably implies that, under special circumstances, the emperor might grant special privileges to one or both of the parties involved in the present conflict. Such imperial enactment might

affect in some way parts of the agreement that has been reached. If the list in our text is not simply a catalogue of theoretical possibilities, then the implication is that the imperial court at Constantinople could somehow interfere in cases such as the present one. It is not unlikely that such involvement could be procured through a petition by one of the parties, but there is no explicit mention of it in our text. It seems that even after the settlement was signed one of the parties could still try to go to the imperial capital and appeal to the emperor. If the emperor was willing to grant a retroactive ἄφεϲιϲ, such an act would affect (a) the payment ὑπὲρ λυτρώϲεωϲ ὑποθήκηϲ, and (b) the payment of the debt. Even the possibility of such imperial interference, however unlikely it may seem, is excluded beforehand. For parallels for the phrase, see, e.g., *Cod. Just.* I 3, 35 (βαϲιλικὴ φιλοτιμία) and the inscription from Bostra mentioned in *BÉ* 1966, no. 474 (a φιλοτιμία of Justinian), both of which refer to concrete acts of generosity granted by the emperor.

What is implied by this formula may be in the same line of tradition as the φιλάνθρωπα, mentioned in Ptolemaic documents that involved debt, such as loans. These φιλάνθρωπα could be granted by the king and they are mentioned in the documents in the form of an exclusion formula, as θεία φιλοτιμία is in our document and similar expressions in the parallels we cite below. However, whereas the earlier φιλάνθρωπα were of a more general nature, the φιλοτιμία of the later period seems to convey the idea of a more specific action and to be more *ad hominem*. For the φιλάνθρωπα, see L. Koenen, *Eine ptolemäische Königurkunde* (P.Kroll.) (Wiesbaden, 1957), especially pp. 1-3.

The other extant settlements of dispute contain the following expressions in this particular section of the agreement: ὑπὸ θείου γράμματοϲ (**#22**, 19); μήτε διὰ {ρ}ῥεϲκρίπτου (see later on in our text) μήτε [διὰ] θείαϲ ἀδνοτατίονοϲ (**#22**, 33-34); διὰ θείων βέρβων (**#29**, 71); θείαϲ ἀδνουτατίωνοϲ (**#29**, 85); and διὰ βαϲιλικῆϲ ἀντιγραφῆϲ (**#32**, 52).

πραγματικοῦ τύπου: "imperial decree." This corresponds to the expression *pragmatica sanctio* that we find in Latin legal texts from the later Roman period, such as *Novellae* VI 9. See Lewis & Short, *A Latin Dictionary* s.v. *pragmatica* B II. H.G. Heumann & E. Seckel, *Heumanns Handlexikon zu den Quellen des römischen Rechts* (9th ed. Jena, 1907), gloss this expression in the following way: "kaiserliches Reskript an eine Korporation, Beamtenschaft, Gemeinde oder Provinz in Angelegenheiten des öffentlichen Rechts." See also E. Schönbauer, "Pragmatica Sanctio," *FF* 35 (1961): 179-83 for a summary of the evidence for *pragmatica sanctio.*

ῥεϲκρίπτου: this is the only word of Latin origin (*rescriptum*) used in our text. A rescript is an indirect kind of imperial legislation. See A. Berger, op. cit. (note to lines 40-41) s.v. *rescripta principum.* It refers to a pronouncement by an emperor made at the request of individual Roman citizens or communities or officials. This distinguishes it from the next item in the formula of our text. For the evolution of rescripts into regular law, see D. Nörr, "Zur Reskriptenpraxis in der hohen Prinzipatszeit." *ZSS* 98 (1981): 1-46. The later rescripts that were found in Aphrodito (*P.Cair.Masp.* I 67024-9) also deal with a variety of administrative problems, such as conflicts over the sphere of competence of various officials who attempted to meddle in the affairs of the town. *P.Cair.Masp.* I 67032 is a very interesting document, because it shows how a rescript, once obtained, can be enforced at the local level only by suing the party that does not abide by its decision. See on this text the references in J.G. Keenan, "On Law and Society in Late Roman Egypt," *ZPE* 17 (1975): 246.

65-66. θείου νεύματοϲ: "imperial will." An imperial *numen* might have repercussions on the agreement reached by the parties in a number of ways, just as a rescript might do. In general, the imperial *numen,* through direct legislation, may alter the options for legal action available in a particular conflict. An imperial *numen* is already mentioned in a papyrus as early as A.D. 293/305. In *P.Lips.* 44 II 12 the edition reads: *ex n[umine n]ostro.* In the republication in *Ch.L.A.* XII 526 the supplement *n[umine* is rejected for reasons of space (*n[...*). Not surprisingly, *n[utu* is a good alternative to *n[umine,* and it is probably the correct reading. See H.G. Heumann & E. Seckel, op. cit. (note to line 65) s.v. *nutus.*

For a recent survey of the various kinds of legislation in late antiquity, see D. Liebs, "Das Gesetz im spätrömischen Recht," *Das Gesetz in Spätantike und frühem Mittelalter: 4. Symposion der Kommission "Die Funktion des Gesetzes in Geschichte und Gegenwart"* (Göttingen, 1992): 11-27.

66. δικανικῆϲ λεπτολογίαϲ: "judicial or forensic argumentation" or the interpretation of the intricacies of existing law by legal advisers or lawyers (δικανικοί). In a contemporary document, *P.Cair.Masp.* I 57151, 201, this expression (spelled δεκ-) occurs in combination with ὁ τῶν ῥητόρων

cυλλογιcμόc. The translation of this passage offered by the *WB* s.v. λεπτολογία, "Spitzfindigkeit der Anwälte," is too negative.

66-67. ἑτέραc οἱαcδήποτε αἰτίαc cυμβῇ ταύτην ἀτονῆcαι: literally "on whatever other basis this (agreement) or part of it might become ineffective," but in English it would make better sense to translate it as "irrespective of whether this agreement, etc." Here οἱοcδήποτε starts a drastically shortened relative sentence with a verb in the subjunctive. The other occurrences of οἱοcδήποτε in this text are all found within a compacted construction that involves only a substantive and not a more extended relative clause involving a verb; see lines 49, 58, and 68. The entire relative clause functions as a general form of exclusion and acts as a barrier to any other theoretical or practical possibility that is not contained in the preceding genitives. ἄν after οἱοcδήποτε followed by a subjunctive is found only in epic poetry; see *LSJ* s.v. ἄν A II.

The demonstrative ταύτην ("this") refers literally to the document at hand, which was mentioned explicitly for the first and last time in line 31. Note that ταύτην is the subject of the infinitive ἀτονῆcαι, which is itself dependent on the impersonal expression cυμβῇ. The intransitive verb ἀτονέω has the technical meaning "to become ineffective" here, which is occasionally found in Greek legal sources of the later Roman period. See, e.g., Theophilus Antecessor II 16 and III 1, 7, where a will is said to be "rendered invalid." In two passages in Syrianus, Scholia ad Hermogenis status (C. Walz, *Rhetores graeci* IV 790, 2 and 796, 6-7) ἄτονοc and ἀτονωτέρα are used to characterize μετάληψιc, a legal objection, as being ineffective or less effective. This particular meaning of the verb ἀτονέω is ultimately derived from the metaphorical usage of the verb, which means "to become weak, ineffective" when it is used for inanimate objects or abstract nouns. In such a sense the verb is used as early as [Longinus] 11, 2 (probably first century A.D.). Because of its literal meaning, it is not surprising that the word occurs most frequently in medical writers.

ἢ μέρουc αὐτῆc: "or part of it." The first genitive is a scribal error for μέροc.

67-76: ἀλλὰ καὶ ἐcβέcθαι μοι | καθ' ὑμῶν καὶ κατὰ τῶν ὑμῶν κληρονόμων οἱανδήποτε ἀγωγὴν | εἰc πρόcωπον ἢ εἰc πρᾶγμα ὡc ἀνωτέρω εἴρηται διὰ τὸ μηδεμίαν |70| μετουϲίαν ἔχων τοῦ λοιποῦ πρὸϲ ὑμᾶϲ περί τε τοῦ αὐτοῦ κτήματοϲ | ἢ περὶ νομῆϲ τούτου ἢ περὶ χρέουϲ ἢ περὶ ἑτέρου τινὸϲ πράγματοϲ | ἀνήκοντοϲ τῷ αὐτῷ κτήματι καὶ πᾶν αὐτοῦ δίκαιον (read: παντὸϲ αὐτοῦ δικαίου) τὸ ϲύνολον | διὰ τὸ ἐμὲ εἰληφέναι ἐκ πλήρουϲ τὰ δόξαντα δίδοϲθαί μοι πρὸϲ | τὴν κρίϲιν τῶν μέϲων φίλων, τουτέϲτιν νομίϲματα ἑπτὰ παρὰ κεράτια |75| δεκατέϲϲαρα χρυϲοχοϊκῷ ϲταθμῷ καὶ ϲίτου ἀρτάβαϲ εἴκοϲι ὡϲ πολλάκιϲ | εἴρηται

67. ἐϲβέϲθαι μοι: this verb is used in the meaning "to be rendered extinct, to be extinguished" in legal documents of the later Roman period in expressions very similar to ours. The following dative is "ethical" and does not denote the agent; for this, see **#11**, 18 (an early case; A.D. 439); **#22**, 35; **#23**, 43; **#29**, 87; **#35**, 20; and *SB* III 7033, 45 and 67. Cf. also the expression ϲβέϲιϲ δίκηϲ in *P.Lond.* V 1708, 248, which L.S.B. MacCoull, *Dioscorus of Aphrodito: His Work and His World* (Berkeley, 1988) 34 would like to read as a metaphor, the lawsuit being like "fire raging in society."

70. μετουϲίαν: "part" or "share" in the legal right of ownership. A partnership in this sense might be no more than having some legal claim on property used to secure a loan by the real owner.

72. πᾶν αὐτοῦ δίκαιον: "every legal right." This expression should have been in the genitive, because it depends on περί as much as the other items in lines 70-72.

75-76. ὡϲ πολλάκιϲ εἴρηται: a nice touch; the scribe is aware of his repetitiousness, which he nevertheless employs for good reasons.

(iv) *Oath sworn in the name of the emperor* (76-81)

76-81: καὶ προϲεπὶ τούτοιϲ πᾶϲι καὶ ἐφ' ἑκάϲτῳ τῶν προγεγραμμένων | κεφαλαίων ἐπωμοϲάμην τήν τε ἁγίαν καὶ ὁμοούϲιον τριάδα καὶ | τὴν εὐϲέβειαν καὶ νίκην τοῦ καλλινίκου δεϲπότου τῆϲ οἰκουμένηϲ | Φλ(αουίου) Ἰουϲτινιανοῦ τοῦ αἰωνίου αὐγούϲτου αὐτοκράτοροϲ ἐμμένειν |80| διηνεκῶϲ τῇ δυνάμει ταύτης τῆς διαλυτικῆς ὁμολογίας καὶ | παντὶ μέρει αὐτῆς καὶ κεφαλαίῳ καὶ κατὰ μηδένα τρόπον παραβῆναι

76. προςεπὶ τούτοις πᾶςι: "for all this in general." It is best here to take προςεπί as equivalent to the following ἐφ' and connect both prepositions with the verb ἐπωμοςάμην. In other texts προςεπί is also used as a preposition in its own right; see *P.Oxy.* LIV 3756, 13 n. This tendency to use double prepositions is attested already from the Ptolemaic period onwards. The adverbial πρός is found very rarely in papyri and it hardly exists in the late period; see Preisigke, *WB* s.v. πρός. In one instance (**#23**, 44) the word πρός is taken as an adverb in the context of an oath and the editors translate πρὸς ἐπὶ τούτοις together as "ausserdem" instead of having the expression refer to the object of the oath.

76-77. ἐφ' ἑκάςτῳ τῶν προγεγραμμένων κεφαλαίων: here κεφάλαιον means "item" and is thus used in its proper sense as it is in **#20**, 275. On the later development of κεφάλαιον, which came to mean no more than πρᾶγμα, see D. Tabachovitz, *Études sur le grec de la basse époque* (Uppsala, 1943) 64-65.

77-79. τήν τε ἁγίαν καὶ ὁμοούςιον τριάδα καὶ τὴν εὐςέβειαν καὶ νίκην τοῦ καλλινίκου δεςπότου τῆς οἰκουμένης Φλ(αουίου) Ἰουςτινιανοῦ τοῦ αἰωνίου αὐγούςτου αὐτοκράτορος: "by the holy and consubstantial Trinity and the piety and victory of the gloriously triumphant lord of the world, Flavius Justinianus, the eternal august emperor." The exact wording of this oath formula is found only in *SB* V 8029, 23 from Antinoopolis, dating from the year A.D. 537. In conjuction with other considerations regarding the career of Apollos (see the introduction, section 5), it is legitimate to speculate that 537 was also the date of our papyrus. It is worth noting that the formula recorded in our papyrus (with the addition τὸν θεῖον καὶ ςεβάςμιον ὅρκον before τήν τε) is typical of documents drawn up in Antinoopolis. See the relevant examples listed by K.A. Worp, "Byzantine Imperial Titulature in the Greek Documentary Papyri: The Oath Formulas," *ZPE* 45 (1982): 211 (section g).

As to the dating formula at the beginning of the papyrus, which is now lost, one can assume that it referred only to the consuls (or a post-consulate) and the indiction. This practice, which was common in Egypt, was changed on August 31, A.D. 537, when Justinian issued *Novella* XXXXVII, ordering that documents were to be dated by regnal year, consulate and indiction. The new practice, however, was not implemented instantly. Thus for the Antinoopolite nome, the earliest attestation is for 555. See R.S. Bagnall & K.A. Worp, *Regnal Formulas in Byzantine Egypt* (Missoula, 1979) 45-48.

79-80. ἐμμένειν διηνεκῶϲ τῇ δυνάμει: "to abide forever by the legal force." This particular combination of words is also found in *P.Mich.* XIII 665, 90.

(v) *Penalty clause* (82-96)

82-88: εἰ δέ ποτε καιρῷ ἢ χρόνῳ τολμήϲαιμι παραβῆναι πάντα τὰ διομολο|γηθέντα παρ' ἐμοῦ ἐν ταύτῃ τῇ διαλυτικῇ ὁμολογίᾳ καὶ βουληθείην | ὑπεναντίον τι χωρεῖν, ὁμολογῶ παραϲχεῖν ὑμῖν λόγῳ προϲτίμου |[85]| ἐπὶ μόνου τοῦ ἐπιχειρήματοϲ τῆϲ παραβάϲεωϲ χρυϲοῦ νομιϲμάτια | εἰκοϲιτέϲϲαρα ἔργῳ καὶ δυνάμει ἀπαιτούμενα πρὸϲ τῷ ὑποκεῖϲθαί με | τῷ τῆϲ ἐπιορκίαϲ (read: ἐπιορκείαϲ) κινδύνῳ καὶ τοῖϲ ὡριϲμένοιϲ κατὰ νόμουϲ ἐπιτιμίοιϲ | κατὰ τῶν παραβαίνειν ἐπιχειρούντων τὰϲ ἐνωμότουϲ ἑαυτῶν ϲυνθήκαϲ

82-83. εἰ . . . τολμήϲαιμι . . . καὶ βουληθείην . . . : "if I should dare . . . and if I should want . . ." The conditional εἰ with optatives is also found in lines 90 and 94. The optative is artificially revived in the Byzantine period after a period of virtual nonexistence. In combination with the optative εἰ and rarely ἐάν are used to express a "possible contingency;" this meaning could also be attained by using the subjunctive or the indicative, which were commonly employed to that end when the optative became obsolete. See R.C. Horn, *The Use of the Subjunctive and Optative Moods in the Non-literary Papyri* (Philadelphia, 1926) 161-70, G. Anlauf, *Standard Late Greek oder Attizismus? Eine Studie zum Optativgebrauch im nachklassischen Griechisch* (Cologne, 1960), especially pp. 114-24 for the non-literary texts, and B.G. Mandilaras, op. cit. (note to line 39) §649.

84. χωρεῖν: this verb here has a technical meaning: "to proceed" in a legal sense. On this, see F.A.J. Hoogendijk & P. van Minnen, "Drei Kaiserbriefe Gordians III an die Bürger von Antinoopolis," *Tyche* 2 (1987): 44, note to

line 8. It occurs in an early settlement of a dispute as well: **#1**, 21, where it is combined with διὰ δίκηc.

λόγῳ προcτίμου: "as a fine." The same expression, equivalent to Latin *poena*, occurs twice in *Cod. Just.* IV 21, 16 and also in *P.Cair.Masp.* III 67299, 56-57; **#26**, 18: λόγῳ προcτίμου παραβάcεωc (3 solidi); **#27**, 29: λόγῳ προcτίμου παραβάcεωc (4.5 solidi); **#35**, 24 (9 solidi); **#25**, 70: λόγῳ ποινῆc (12 solidi); **#29**, 76 (12 solidi); **#30**, 30 and 36 (12 solidi); **#33**, 4: λόγῳ καταδίκηc (12 solidi); **#38**, 4-5 (12 solidi); **#41**, 89-90: λόγῳ προcτίμου καὶ μόνου ("and only on that count"; 12 solidi); *SB* VI 9590, 17 (12 solidi); **#32** (p. 202) 57: λόγῳ προcτίμου καὶ παραβαcίαc (18 solidi); *SB* III 7033, 71 (36 solidi); **#20**, 266 (100 solidi); **#22**, 46 (360 solidi); **#37** (p. 205) 20 and 23 (amount lost); *SB* I 4671, 1: λόγῳ προcτίμου καὶ ποινῆc (6 solidi). As one can see, the amount of the πρόcτιμον varied and was probably dictated by the importance of the case or the value of the disputed object.

The πρόcτιμον, the fine stipulated for breaking the present agreement, is one of the most powerful holds that Phoebammon and Anastasia have over Nicantinous. This stipulation will effectively coerce him to refrain from breaking his written promise and from initiating legal proceedings against them. This explains why Nicantinous highlights this element in his signature (line 102: ἐπὶ τῷ πρωcτίμῳ) and swears an oath. On the importance of the inclusion of a πρόcτιμον in agreements of settlement from the later Roman period, see A. Steinwenter, op.cit. (note to lines 17-18): 91-92 and A. Berger, op. cit. (note to lines 40-41) s.v. *stipulatio poenae.* It is clear that the πρόcτιμον, specified here as 24 solidi, was to be paid to the other party. The recipients of the ἐπιτίμια of line 87, however, were probably the local authorities (see the note to line 87).

86. ἔργῳ καὶ δυνάμει ἀπαιτούμενα: "to be demanded as a matter of fact and with full legal power"; see the note on *P.Münch.* I 4, 35. This formula refers to the collection of the fine, which is to be paid by the party that breaks the agreement. The formula also seems to differentiate the ways in which the fine may be collected in the event of breach of contract. However, the precise meaning of the two terms is not clear and thus the function of this legal provision is rather obscure. The term δυνάμει probably refers to some form of legal action that may be taken to enforce the payment of the fine, whereas ἔργῳ might actually imply that the fine will be collected in person, "as a matter of fact," by the party who is entitled to collect the fine. In our case, the fine would be collected by

Phoebammon and Anastasia. Only if the party responsible for breaking the agreement refuses to pay the fine will δύναμις have to come into play. This idea finds support in the order in which the terms are listed in the formula: ἔργον first, δύναμις as a last resort, so to speak. There might, however, be an altogether different notion implied by the expression: if one of the parties does not abide by the agreement, the other party can either collect the fine and "really" get the money in cash, or start legal proceedings threatening the collection of the money, but not necessarily collecting any in the end. In that case δυνάμει could be rendered as "potentially."

For parallels in a similar context, see **#20**, 267-268; **#21**, 40-41; **#25**, 71 and 14, 77-78; **#26**, 19-20; **#27**, 29; *P.Cair.Masp.* I 67032, 81-82. Cf. also *SB* III 7033, 47: τούτων τοίνυν ἔργῳ καὶ δυνάμει γεγενημένων, which is also a settlement of a dispute **#15)**.

πρὸς τῷ: here unlike in line 39 the dative is properly used in the meaning "in addition to." Paying the πρόστιμον for breach of contract does not free the offender from the charge of perjury. Additionally, the fine for breaking a contract still needs to be paid to the government (see the note on the next line). On πρὸς τῷ + infinitive meaning "besides," see B.G. Mandilaras, op. cit. (note to line 39) §861 (5).

87. τοῖς ὡρισμένοις κατὰ νόμοις ἐπιτιμίοις: "the penalties stipulated by the laws." For direct parallels for this phrase, see **#32** (p. 202) 56-57, and **#37** (p. 205) 17-18 and 53. There are many references to ἐπιτίμια in later Roman laws. See M. San Nicolò, *Vocabularium Codicis Iustiniani*, Vol. 2 (Prague, 1925) s.v. ἐπιτίμια. The ἐπιτίμια could vary depending on the importance of the case. Often they are double the value of the property involved in the contract. According to texts from eighth-century Thebes, the penalty between family members for breaking an agreement was 36 solidi (in *P.Cair.Masp.* III 67299, 57-58 the πρόστιμον to be paid to the other party also happens to be 36 solidi). These fines had to be paid to the proper authorities as a *Fiskalmult*. See the references in W.C. Till, *Erbrechtliche Untersuchungen aufgrund der koptischen Urkunden* (Wien, 1953) 25. On the Latin equivalent cf. A. Berger, op. cit. (note to lines 40-41) s.v. *multa*.

88. συνθήκας: "agreements." For a parallel, see **#32** (p. 202) 57: ἐνομότους (read ἐνωμότους) συνθήκας.

89-96: οὐδὲν δὲ ⟨ἧττον⟩ καὶ πρὸ τοῦ προϲτίμου καὶ μετὰ τὴν τοῦ προϲτίμου καταβολήν, | εἴ ποτε πρὸϲ ἀπαίτηϲιν ἁρμόϲοι, ἀρραγῆ καὶ ἀϲάλευτον εἶναι ταύτην | τὴν διαλυτικὴν ὁμολογίαν διὰ παντὸϲ ἥνπερ ὑμῖν ἐθέμην | πρὸϲ ἀϲφάλειαν κυρίαν οὖϲαν καὶ βεβαίαν ὑποθέμενοϲ ὑμῖν | εἰϲ ἅπαντα τὰ προγεγραμμένα καὶ εἰϲ τὴν τοῦ προϲτίμου ἀπαίτηϲιν, | εἰ οὕτω τύχοι, πάντα τὰ νῦν ὄντα μοι καὶ ἐϲόμενα πράγματα κινητά τε | καὶ ἀκίνητα καὶ αὐτοκίνητα ἐνεχύρου λόγῳ καὶ ὑποθήκηϲ | δικαίῳ καθάπερ ἐκ δίκηϲ

89. οὐδὲν δὲ ⟨ἧττον⟩: the sentence structure requires the insertion of ἧττον. For a good parallel, see **#20**, 270-71.

καὶ πρὸ τοῦ προϲτίμου καὶ μετὰ τὴν τοῦ προϲτίμου καταβολήν: the first part of this phrase seems overcautious, but in all likelihood we are dealing yet with one more instance of a polar expression (see also notes to lines 50, 59, and 62). For a good parallel for the second part of the phrase, see **#32** (p. 202), 61-63: πρὸϲ τῷ καὶ μετὰ τὴν τοῦ προϲτίμου καὶ τῶν ἀναλωμάτων καὶ δαπανημάτων καὶ ζημιωμάτων καταβολὴν ἔχειν ταύτην τὴν ὁμολογίαν τῆϲ διαλύϲεωϲ [τὴν ἰ]δί[α]ν (so rightly *Berichtigungsliste* 1, 234) ἰϲχύν.

90. ἁρμόϲοι: "befalls" *vel sim*. The meaning of the verb here is different from the one that we have encountered in line 59 (see the note there). We are apparently dealing with a case of the future optative here as well as in **#20**, 279, where the editor thinks ἁρμόϲοι stands for ἁρμόζοι, and **#41**, 91: εἰ πρὸϲ ἀπαίτηϲιν ἁρμόϲοι. On the future optative, which is very rarely used in Greek, see the references in S.E. Porter, *Verbal Aspect in the Greek of the New Testament with Reference to Tense and Mood* (New York, 1989) 409. In later Greek a future optative form was occasionally invented by analogy.

ἀρραγῆ καὶ ἀϲάλευτον: the combination of these two adjectives occurs also in **#21**, 41-42 and *SB* III 7033, 73.

92. ὑποθέμενοϲ: "while I put up as security." The object follows in lines 94-95.

94. εἰ οὕτω τύχοι: "if it ever happens so." For a parallel, see **#29**, 98, and for the formulaic use of the optative in this type of hypothetical clause, see R.C. Horn, op. cit. (note to lines 82-83) 161.

95. αὐτοκίνητα: literally this word means "self-movers" and, then, by extension, "livestock" including slaves. The word, common in papyri, is also mentioned in relation to property used to secure a loan in *Novella* CXII 1: ὥϲτε εἰ μὲν ἰδικὰ πράγματα κινητὰ ἢ ἀκίνητα ἢ αὐτοκίνητα ὀνομαςτὶ ταῖϲ ὑποθήκαιϲ ἐμφέροιτο κ.τ.λ. It corresponds to the distinction made in Roman law among *res mobiles*, *immobiles* and *se moventes*. The last-mentioned expression was added only in the fifth century A.D. See A. Berger, op. cit. (note to lines 40-41) s.v. *res se moventes*. In Greek it is also used in, e.g., *Cod. Just.* I 3, 43, 4, of A.D. 530, where it is combined with πράγματα as here. For parallels in papyri, see **#30**, 10 and 14; **#35**, 14; and **#37** (p. 206) 61.

95-96. ἐνεχύρου λόγῳ καὶ ὑποθήκηϲ δικαίῳ: "as a pledge and with the legal right of security." For parallels, see **#21**, 49; **#29**, 97; **#31**, 57; **#32** (p. 202), 69; and **#37** (p. 206) 61-62.

96. καθάπερ ἐκ δίκηϲ: "as if ruled by court," i.e., with the same legal force as if it were a court decision. See H.J. Wolff "Some Observations on Praxis," *Proc. Twelfth Intern. Congr. Papyr.* (Toronto, 1970): 527-35. This usually rather meaningless phrase is exceptionally apt in this case, because the parties to the dispute seriously considered taking the matter to court–and were actually in the courthouse in Aphrodito when they reached an agreement.

(vi) *Clause validating the agreement* (96-98)

96-98: καὶ εἰϲ τὰ προγεγραμμένα πάντα | ἐπερωτηθεὶϲ παρ' ὑμῶν ταῦθ' οὕτωϲ ἔχειν, δώϲειν, ποιεῖν, φυλάττειν, | ἐμμένειν, πληρώϲειν, εἰϲ πέραϲ ἄγειν ὡμολόγηϲα

97-98. ἐπερωτηθεὶϲ παρ' ὑμῶν . . . ὡμολόγηϲα: "having been asked the formal question by you . . . I acknowledged." For this formula, known as *stipulatio*, see the study by D. Simon, *Untersuchungen zur Praxis der Stipulationsklausel* (Munich, 1964).

ταῦθ' οὕτωϲ ἔχειν, δώϲειν, ποιεῖν, φυλάττειν, ἐμμένειν, πληρώϲειν, εἰϲ πέραϲ ἄγειν: "that this is so, that I shall give it, that I do it, keep it, abide by it, that I shall fulfil it, that I bring it to an end." For more or less close parallels in settlements of dispute and documents of kindred nature, see **#20**, 276-77; **#29**, 85; *P.Cair.Masp.* I 67032, 84-85; II 67156, 33-34; and *SB* III 7033, 75-76. For references to this formula in contracts of sale from late Roman Aphrodito, see *P.Vat.Aphrod.* 4, 14 n. The infinitives vary in tense, but, by some coincidence, they all end in -ειν. This might have been done on purpose by the scribe for the sake of rhetorical artistry (homoioteleuton). Note also the crescendo in the number of syllables of the infinitives. For the phrase εἰϲ πέραϲ ἄγειν, see also *P.Cair.Masp.* I 67032, 59 and 65-66.

Signatures and subscription (98-116)

98-103: Αὐρήλιοϲ Νικαντίνοοϲ | Ἰϲιδώρου ὁ προγεγραμμένοϲ ἐθέμην ταύτην τὴν διαλυτικὴν |[100]| ὁμολογίαν ἒϲ΄χηκὸϲ (read: ἐϲχηκώϲ) ἐκ πλήρουϲ τὰ δόξαντα, τουτέϲτιν | νομιϲμάτια ἑπτὰ καὶ ϲίτου ἀρτάβαϲ εἴκοϲει (read: εἴκοϲι), καὶ ὄμιϲα (read: ὤμοϲα) | τὸν θεῖον ὅρκον ἐπὶ τῷ πρωϲτίμῳ (read: προϲτίμῳ) καὶ πίθωμαι (read: πείθομαι) πᾶϲι τοῖϲ | ἐγγεγραμμένοιϲ ὡϲ πρόκ(ειται) καὶ ὑπογράψαϲ ἀπέλυϲα

Nicantinous writes clearly legible Greek. He makes a few mistakes in the spelling of some words.

101. ὄμιϲα: "I swore the oath." The interchange of ο > ι in ὤμοϲα and similar forms is unparalleled.

103. ἀπέλυϲα: "I have released it." The technical meaning of the verb here is "to absolve" (a document) or "to hand it over," equivalent to Latin *absolvere.* See *P.Münch.* I 3, 10 n. as well as A. Berger, "Miscellanea Papyrologica," *JJP* 1 (1946): 37 for references to legal discussions of the term.

103-6: Αὐρ(ήλιοϲ) | Μουϲῆϲ Ψαίου ϲυντελεϲτὴϲ ἀπὸ τῆϲ ὰὐ΄τῆϲ κώμηϲ Ἀφροδίτηϲ |[105]| εὑρεθεὶϲ ἐν Ἀντινόου μαρτυρῶ τῇ ὁμολογίᾳ{ν} ἤτοι διαλύcει | ἀκούcαc παρὰ τοῦ θεμένου

Muses writes clearly legible Greek. He makes one grammatical mistake. For the implications of the presence of witnesses to this kind of contract, see our introduction, section 3.

104. Μουcῆc Ψαίου: this man also signs as a witness in *P.Hamb.* III 234, 14-15. The identity of the hand can be established on the basis of the plate.

105. εὑρεθείc: "currently, being presently." The verb εὑρίcκομαι has a meaning here that is equivalent to German "sich befinden."

ὁμολογίᾳ{ν} ἤτοι διαλύcει: "the agreement or settlement." On this meaning of ἤτοι, see P.J. Sijpesteijn, "The Meaning of ἤτοι in the Papyri," *ZPE* 90 (1992): 242. Technically speaking the document is a διαλυτικὴ ὁμολογία (see lines 91, 99-100, 108, 110 and 112). See also the note on line 113.

ἀκούcαc: all the witnesses state that they heard the reading of the present document and Nicantinous' oral agreement. This was apparently more important than reading his immediately preceding signature.

106-8: Ἑρμαῶc Βόττου ἀπὸ τῆc αὐτῆc | κώμηc Ἀφροδίτηc εὑρεθεὶc ἐν Ἀντινόου μαρτυρῶ τῇ | διαλυτικῇ ὁμολογίᾳ ἀκούcαc παρὰ τοῦ θεμένου

Hermaos is the second witness to sign the document. All the wintesses, like him and Muses above, write in legible and flawless Greek.

106. Ἑρμαῶc Βόττου: for this man, see also *P.Cair.Masp.* I 67001, 47 of A.D. 514, where he also acts as a witness. Note that he leaves out Αὐρήλιοc before his name here, but not in the other text. We do not, however, have to assume that Hermaos was a clergyman or a monk by the time this text was written. On the habit of leaving out Αὐρήλιοc in the case of such people, see the note on line 1a. If Hermaos was a clergyman, this would have been indicated in some way in the subscription, e.g., by a title, such as πρεcβύτεροc.

108-10: Αὐρήλιοc | Cενούθηc Ἀπολλῶτοc ἀπὸ τῆc αὐτῆc κώμηc Ἀφροδίτηc εὑρεθεὶc |[110]| ἐν Ἀντινόου μαρτυρῶ τῇ διαλυτικῇ ὁμολογίᾳ ἀκούcαc παρὰ τοῦ θεμένου

For the signature of Senuthes, see the note to line 108-110.

109. Cενούθηc Ἀπολλῶτοc: this presumably older brother of Dioscorus also occurs as a witness in a number of other texts. See the references in the introduction to **#20**.

111-12: Αὐρήλιοc Ἀπολλῶc Βηcίου ἀπὸ τῆc αὐτῆc κώμηc Ἀφρ[ο]δίτηc εὑρ[εθεὶ]c | ἐν Ἀντιν̣όου μ[αρτυ]ρ[ῶ τῇ δ]ιαλ̣[υτ]ι̣κ̣ῇ ὁμ̣ο̣λ̣ογί[ᾳ ἀκού]cαc παρὰ τοῦ θεμ̣έ̣[νου].

For the signature of this man, see note to line 108-110.

111. Ἀπολλῶc Βηc̣ίου: this man also occurs as a witness in *P.Flor.* III 280, 26-27, which dates from A.D. 514. Unfortunately no plate of this text was published so that we cannot compare the hands. This Apollos is mentioned in other texts as well, one of which dates to 533/534 at the latest. See the references in J. Gascou & L.S.B. MacCoull, op. cit. (note to line 15) 140, note on line 131.

113: Φ[̣] ̣[̣] ̣[̣ ̣] ̣τα ̣ ου κ̣[ ]ηθ̣[. . . .] ̣ ̣τ̣[. . .]. . . .λ[. . . .]δ ̣ ̣[. . . . .] ̣ ἀκ̣ο̣ύ̣[c]α̣c̣ πα̣ρὰ το̣ῦ̣ θ̣εμ̣έ̣[ν̣ου] ̣

113. This line may, e.g., be restored as follows: Φ[ιλ]ή̣[μω]ν̣ [Ἀνα]c̣ταc̣ίου κ̣[λ]ηθ̣[εὶc μ]α̣ρ̣τ̣[υρῶ τ]ῇ ὁ̣μ̣ο̣λ[ογίᾳ] δ̣ι̣α̣[λύcεω]c̣ ἀ̣κ̣ο̣ύ̣[c]α̣c̣ π̣α̣ρὰ τ̣ο̣ῦ θεμ̣έ[νου]: "I, Philemon, son of Anastasius, called upon (to witness), witness the agreement of settlement, after having heard it from the man who made it." The trace following the first lacuna belongs to either an eta or a kappa. Something like Φ[λ(άουιοc)] Ἥ̣[ρω]ν̣ is equally possible. The only certain piece of information about this individual is that the man did not have Αὐρήλιοc before his name. The reading of the central part of the line is difficult because of severe abrasion of the ink. Reading τ]ῇ

would be fine, because the trace following the lacuna belongs to one of the long letters, but there seems to be too much space between ὁ̣μ̣ο̣- and the following lambda. Moreover, the space seems too small for μ]α̣ρ̣τ̣[υρῶ τ]ῇ. It is possible that μ]ά̣ρ̣τ̣[υϲ was written instead of μ]α̣ρ̣τ̣[υρῶ. The expression κ̣[λ]η̣θ[εὶϲ μ]ά̣ρ̣τ̣[υϲ occurs nowhere else, but for the idea of "calling" a witness it suffices to refer to *P.Hal.* 1, 225 and 231. It would, however, be odd to find a signature without a verb.

In this line we are probably dealing with a witness from Antinoopolis, because the signature, whatever it was, seems to be quite different from that of the four preceding witnesses. This does not necessarily imply that this witness was summoned simply from the middle of the street. He might have been a friend of one of the two parties who happened to live in Antinoopolis. This may explain why he does not mention his place of origin as the others do. The witnesses who sign their names in lines 103-112 are all from Aphrodito and are probably to be identified with some or all of the friends who act as mediators between the disputing parties. At least they came from the same village as the parties to the conflict. In the two lines that follow there is room for one or two more signatures.

116. In the last line on the papyrus we may recognize the signature of the notary (reading δι' ἐ]μ̣[οῦ). It cannot be established beyond doubt that the last line is indented, as it should be in the case of a notary's signature, nor that it really was the last line of the document. But since the papyrus is broken off at the top, the lower end of the papyrus must have been inside the roll when it was found. Not much papyrus can therefore be lost at the end. In our opinion there were either six or seven witnesses. The number of witnesses varies greatly in settlements of dispute from the later Roman period.

Table 1. List of Late Antique Settlements in Greek

Throughout this monograph the following settlements are referred to by the number in boldface type only. This will immediately signal readers that the text referred to is a settlement. For some of the terminology used see the Introduction, section 9. Source: the appropriate entries in the *WB* and the materials in the Duke Data Bank of Documentary Papyri.

	Text	Date	Provenance	Called
1	*P.Oxy.* XII 1562	A.D. 276-282	Oxyrhynchus	διάλυϲιϲ
	dispute about property rights to a house under lien (?)			
	initiated by the buyer (the seller is a councillor of Oxyrhynchus)			
	settled through arbitration by an official			
2	*P.Stras.* IV 280	3d cent. A.D.	Hermopolis	ἀνεγκληϲία
	dispute about ?			
	initiated by both parties, one of whom is a daughter of a councillor of Hermopolis			
	settled through ? preceded by petitions to officials			
3	*P.Oxy.* XXXVI 2768	3d cent. A.D.	Oxyrhynchus	?
	dispute about property rights			
	initiated by a woman			
	settled through mediation preceded by joinder of issue			
4	*PSI* XII 1256	3d cent. A.D.	Oxyrhynchus	?
	dispute about property rights through inheritance			
	initiated by both parties, one of whom is a veteran			
	settled through mediation preceded by petitions to officials			

	Text	Date	Provenance	Called
5	*P.Berl.Möller* 1	A.D. 300	Euergetis	περίλυϲιϲ

dispute about a deposit of money
initiated by both parties, two women
settled through negotiation preceded by joinder of issue

6	*P.Princ.* II 79	A.D. 326	Oxyrhynchus	διάλυϲιϲ

dispute about property rights to land through inheritance
initiated by three brothers
settled through ?

7	*PSI* VIII 951	A.D. 388 ?	?	διάλυϲιϲ

dispute about ?
initiated by a freedman
settled through ? preceded by a petition to the prefect

8	*P.Lips.* 14	A.D. 391	Hermopolis	διάλυϲιϲ

dispute about a loan of money
initiated by the creditor of a wool merchant
settled through negotiation preceded by a petition to the prefect

9	*P.Haun.* III 57	A.D. 412-415 ?	?	διάλυϲιϲ

dispute about personal damages
initiated by an official (the other party is a higher official)
settled through mediation preceded by a petition to the prefect

10	*P.Oxy.* XVI 1880	A.D. 427	Oxyrhynchus	διάλυϲιϲ

dispute about ?
initiated by an Alexandrian merchant (the other party is also an Alexandrian merchant)
settled through ? preceded by a petition to an official

11	*CPR* VI 6	A.D. 439	Hermopolis	διάλυϲιϲ

dispute about property rights to land (preceded by a sale of land: *Stud.Pal.* XX 121)
initiated by the buyer, an official
settled through ?

	Text	Date	Provenance	Called
12	*P.Flor.* III 311	A.D. 447	Hermopolis	?

dispute about ?
initiated by a donkey-driver (the other party is his employer, a *scholastikos* ?)
settled through negotiation preceded by a petition

13	*SB* XIV 11896	A.D. 425-455	Hermopolis	διάλυϲιϲ

dispute about ?
initiated by ?
settled through mediation by a *scholastikos* ?

14	*PSI* X 1114	A.D. 454	Oxyrhynchus?	διάλυϲιϲ

dispute about ?
initiated by ?
settled through ? preceded by a petition to the the prefect

15	*P.Princ.* II 82 + *SB* III 7033	A.D. 481	Lycopolis	διάλυϲιϲ

dispute about property rights to movables (clothes)
initiated by a bishop and two priests (the other party is their deacon)
settled through mediation preceded by a petition

16	*SB* I 5941	A.D. 510	?	?

dispute about property rights to a house
initiated by the buyer, a school-teacher (the other party is the seller, a linen-merchant)
settled through mediation

17	*Tyche* 5 (1990) 85-91	A.D. 511 ?	Arsinoe	διάλυϲιϲ

dispute about property rights to a monastic cell
initiated by a Meletian monk (the other party is another monk)
settled through ?

18	*P.Vat.Aphrod.* 10 + P.Mich.inv. 6922	A.D. 537 ?	Aphrodito	διάλυϲιϲ

dispute about property rights to land under lien
initiated by the representative of the buyers
settled through mediation

	Text	Date	Provenance	Called
19	*P.Lond.* III 1008 (p. 265)	A.D. 561	?	διάλυϲιϲ

dispute about ?
initiated by ? (three brothers settle with their sister)
settled through ?

20	*P.Mich.* XIII 659 + *P.Vat.Aphrod.* 17	A.D. 564/565	Aphrodito	διάλυϲιϲ

dispute about property rights to land and a house and movables
initiated by the seller (the other party represents the heirs of a dead clergyman)
settled through arbitration

21	*P.Lond.* V 1717	c. A.D. 566-573	Antinoopolis	διάλυϲιϲ

dispute about a loan of money
initiated by the debtor (the creditor is a woman)
settled through ?

22	*SB* VIII 9763	A.D. 457-74*	Hermopolis	διάλυϲιϲ

dispute about movables and documents relating to immovables
initiated by both parties
settled through ?

23	*P.Münch.* I 1	A.D. 574	Syene	διάλυϲιϲ

dispute about property rights through inheritance
initiated by the brother of two brothers and a sister
settled through mediation

24	*BGU* I 317	A.D. 580/81	Arsinoe	διάλυϲιϲ

dispute about movables (including clothes)
initiated by ? (the other party is a woman)
settled through ?

25	*P.Münch.* I 7	A.D. 583	Antinoopolis	διάλυϲιϲ

dispute about property rights to a house, and a ship
initiated by the husband of a woman (the other party is her brother)
settled through mediation

	Text	Date	Provenance	Called
26	*P.Lond.* V 1728	A.D. 584 or 585	Syene	ἀμερίμνεια

dispute about property rights to land, a house and a ship
initiated by the sister
settled through private negotiations

27	*P.Lond.* V 1731	A.D. 585	Syene	ἀμερίμνεια

dispute about money
initiated by both parties, a mother and daughter
settled through negotiation

28	*SB* VI 9456	A.D. 594	Arsinoe	διάλυϲιϲ ?

dispute about theft
initiated by the thief, a sausage-seller (the other party is his employer, another sausage-seller)
settled through mediation

29	*P.Münch.* I 14	A.D. 594	Syene	διάλυϲιϲ

dispute about property rights to a house through inheritance
initiated by a sailor (the other party is a soldier)
settled through arbitration by a priest

30	*P.Par.* 20	A.D. 599	Panopolis	διάλυϲιϲ

dispute about property rights through inheritance
initiated by both parties, two dealers in purple cloth and their sister
settled through negotiation

31	*P.Cair.Masp.* II 67167	6th cent. A.D.	Antinoopolis	διαλυτικὴ ὁμολογία

dispute about a loan of money
initiated by the creditor (the other party, an official, represents the dead debtor)
settled through negotiation

32	*P.Lond.* I 113.1 (pp. 199 ff.)	6th cent. A.D.	Arsinoe	διάλυϲιϲ

dispute about a sale price
initiated by the seller, a soldier
settled through mediation

	Text	Date	Provenance	Called
33	*P.Stras.* IV 194 *dispute about* ? *initiated by* ? *settled through* ?	6th cent. A.D.	Hermopolis	διάλυσις
34	*CPR* IX 11 *dispute about* ? *initiated by* ? *settled through* ?	6th cent. A.D.	Hermopolis	διαλυτικὴ ὁμολογία
35	*P.Herm.* 31 *dispute about* property rights through inheritance *initiated* by step-brothers and step-sisters *settled through* ?	6th cent. A.D.	Memnoneia	διάλυσις
36	*SB* I 6000 *dispute about* property rights to a house *initiated by* the daughter (the other party is the mother) *settled through* negotiation	6th cent. A.D.	?	διαλυτικὴ ὁμολογία and διάλυσις
37	*P.Lond.* I 113.2 (pp. 204-207) *dispute about* property rights *initiated by* ? *settled through* ?	6th-7th cent.A.D.	Arsinoe	?
38	*Stud.Pal.* III 405 *dispute about* ? *initiated by* ? *settled through* ?	6th-7th cent. A.D.	Heracleopolis	διάλυσις ?
39	*SB* I 2137 *dispute about* ? *initiated by* ? *settled through* ?	6th-7th cent. A.D.	Thebes	?

	Text	Date	Provenance	Called
40	*SB* I 4765 *dispute about* ? *initiated by?* *settled through* ?	Byz.	?	?
41	*SB* VI 8988	A.D. 647	Apollinopolis	Ἀκυλιανὴ διάλυϲιϲ and ἀμερίμνεια

dispute about property rights to a house
initiated by a deacon (the other party is a husband and wife)
settled through arbitration and negotiation (cf. A.A . Schiller, *JARCE* 7 [1968] 79-118; related sale: *SB* VIII 8987)

---

* The chronological misplacement of document **22** in the list came to our attention when the manuscript was in press.

Map 1. Late Antique Egypt (750 x 1,000 square kilometers)

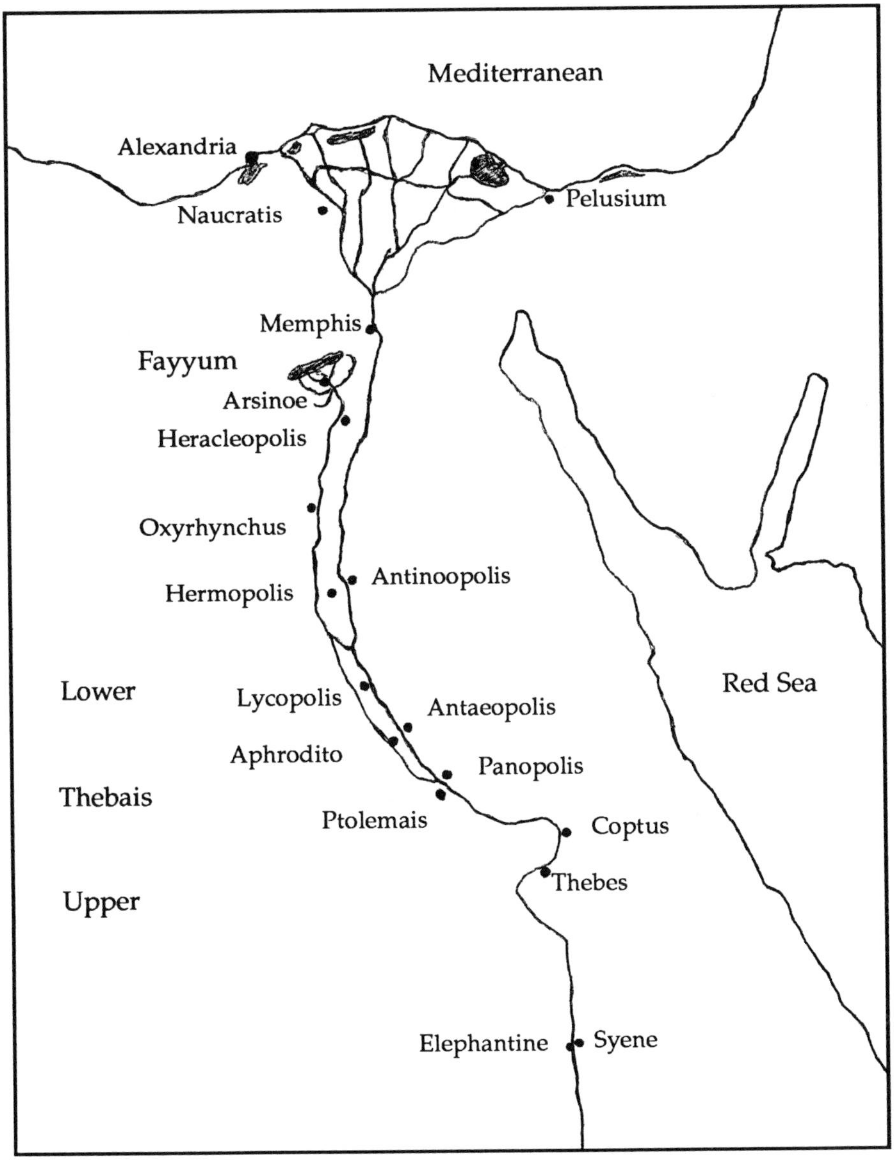

Fig. 1. Family Tree

(women's names are printed in *italics*)

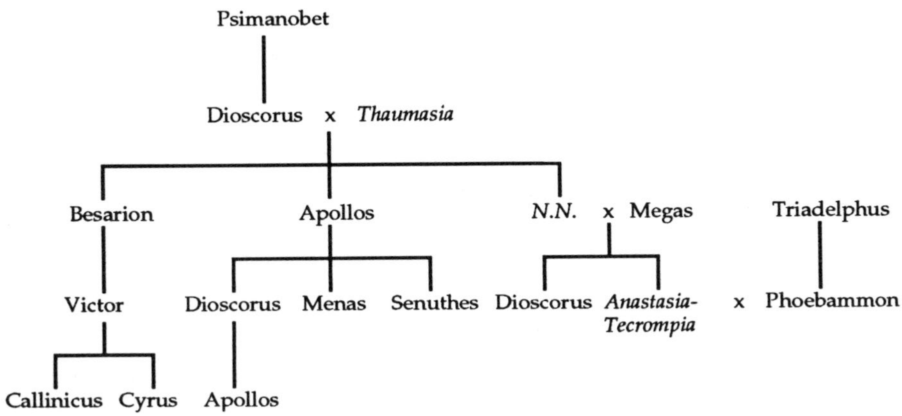

Source: the archives of Dioscorus, son of Apollos, the notary and poet; for Dioscorus, son of Megas, see the note on line 3 in the Commentary.

Bibliography

Papyrus editions (see p. 1, n. 1), standard dictionaries and reviews are not listed.

Allam, S. "Observations on Civil Jurisdiction in Late Byzantine and Early Arabic Egypt." *Life in a Multi-cultural Society: Egypt from Cambyses to Constantine and Beyond*, edited by J.H. Johnson. SAOC, Vol. 51 (Chicago, 1992): 1-8.

Anlauf, G. *Standard Late Greek oder Attizismus? Eine Studie zum Optativgebrauch im nachklassischen Griechisch.* Cologne, 1960.

Arangio-Ruiz, V. *Cours de droit romain (les actions).* Naples, 1935.

Avotins, I. *On the Greek of the Code of Justinian.* Altertumswissenschaftliche Texte und Studien, Vol. 17. Hildesheim, Zürich, & New York, 1989.

Bagnall, R.S. "Two Byzantine Legal Papyri in a Private Collection." In *Studies in Roman Law in Memory of A. Arthur Schiller*, edited by R.S. Bagnall & W.V. Harris. Columbia Studies in the Classical Tradition, Vol. 13 (Leiden, 1986): 1-9.

—. "Church, State and Divorce in Late Roman Egypt." In *Florilegium Columbianum: Essays in Honor of Paul Oskar Kristeller*, edited by K.-L. Selig & R. Somerville. (New York, 1987): 41-61.

—. "Official and Private Violence in Roman Egypt." *BASP* 26 (1989): 201-16.

—. *Egypt in Late Antiquity*. Princeton, 1993.

—, & K.A. Worp. *Regnal Formulas in Byzantine Egypt*. BASP Supplements, Vol. 2. Missoula, 1979.

Bell, H.I. "An Egyptian Village in the Age of Justinian." *JHS* 64 (1944): 21-36.

—. *Egypt from Alexander the Great to the Arab Conquest*. Oxford, 1948.

Berger, A. "Miscellanea Papyrologica." *JJP* 1 (1946): 13-40.

—. *Encyclopedic Dictionary of Roman Law*. Transactions of the American Philosophical Society, Vol. 43.2. Philadelphia, 1953.

Bowersock, G.W. *Hellenism in Late Antiquity*. Ann Arbor, 1990.

Bowman, A.K. "Landholding in the Hermopolite Nome in the Fourth Century." *JRS* 75 (1985): 137-63.

Braunert, H. *Die Binnenwanderung. Studien zur Sozialgeschichte Ägyptens in der Ptolemäer- und Kaiserzeit*. Bonner Historische Forschungen, Vol. 26. Bonn, 1964.

Brown, P. *Society and the Holy in Late Antiquity, A.D. 150-750*. Berkeley, 1982.

Calderini, A. *Dizionario dei nomi geografici dell'Egitto greco-romano*, Vols. 1.1-2. Cairo & Madrid, 1935-66.

—, & S. Daris. *Dizionario dei nomi geografici dell'Egitto greco-romano*, Vols. 2-5 and *Supplemento* 1. Milan, 1973-88.

Cameron, A. "Wandering Poets: A Literary Movement in Byzantine Egypt." *Historia* 14 (1965): 470-509.

Charitonidis, S., L. Kahil, & R. Ginouvès *Les mosaîques de la maison du Ménandre á Mytilène*. Antike Kunst. Beiheft, Vol. 6. Berne, 1970.

Cohoon, J.W. "Rhetorical Studies in the Arbitration Scene of Menander's Epitrepontes." *TAPA* 45 (1914): 141-230.

Comaroff, J.L. & S. Roberts. *Rules and Processes: The Cultural Logic of Dispute in an African Context*. Chicago, 1981.

Davies, W. "Disputes, Their Conduct and Their Settlement in the Village Communities of Eastern Brittany in the Ninth Century." *History and Anthropology* 1 (1985): 289-312.

Decker, W. "Bemerkungen zum Agon für Antinoos in Antinoupolis (Antinoeia)." *Kölner Beiträge zur Sportwissenschaft* 2 (1974): 38-56.

Diethart, J.M. & K.A. Worp. *Notarsunterschriften im byzantinischen Ägypten*. MPER, Vol. 16. Vienna, 1986.

Druffel, E. von. *Papyrologische Studien zum byzantinischen Urkundenwesen im Anschluss an P. Heidelberg 311*. Münch. Beitr., Vol. 1. Munich, 1915.

Ensslin, W. "Ein Prozessvergleich unter Klerikern vom Jahre 481." *RhM* 75 (1926): 422-46.

Farber, J.J. "Family Disputes in the Patermouthis Archive." *BASP* 27 (1991) 111-22.

Fikhman, I.F. *Egipet na rubezhe dvukh epokh. Remeslenniki i remeslennyi trud v IV - seredine VII v.* Moscow, 1965.

——. *Oksirinkh – gorod papirusov*. Moscow & Leningrad, 1976.

——. "De nouveau sur le colonat du Bas Empire." *Miscellanea papyrologica in occasione del bicentenario dell'edizione della Charta Borgiana*, edited by M. Capasso, G. Messeri Savorelli, & R. Pintaudi, Vol. 1. Pap. Flor., Vol. 19.1 (Florence, 1990): 159-79.

Frantz-Murphy, G. "Settlement of Property Disputes in Provincial Egypt: Early Islamic Period." *al-Masâq. Studia Arabo-Islamica Mediterranea* 6 (1993): 95-105.

Gagos, T. & P. van Minnen. "Documenting the Rural Economy of Byzantine Egypt: Three Papyri from Alabastrine." *JRA* 5 (1992): 186-202.

Gascou, J. "Les grands domaines, la cité et l'état en Égypte byzantine." *T&M* 9 (1985): 1-90.

——, & L.S.B. MacCoull. "Le cadastre d'Aphroditô." *T&M* 10 (1987): 103-58.

Gelzer, M. *Studien zur byzantinischen Verwaltung Ägyptens*. Leipziger Historische Abhandlungen, Vol. 13. Leipzig, 1909.

Girgis, V.A. *Prosopografia e Afroditopolis*. Berlin, 1938.

Goitein, S.D. *A Mediterranean Society: The Jewish Communities of the Arab World as Portrayed in the Documents of the Cairo Geniza*, Vol. 2. Berkeley, 1978.

Gronewald, M. "Der neue Poseidippos und Kallimachos Epigramm 35." *ZPE* 99 (1993): 28-29.

Häge, G. "Die μὴ ἐλαττουμένου-Klausel in den griechischen Papyri Ägyptens." In *Proceedings of the Twelfth International Congress of Papyrology*, edited by D.H. Samuel. ASP, Vol. 7 (Toronto, 1970): 195-205.

Hardy, E.R. *The Large Estates of Byzantine Egypt*. Studies in History, Economics and Public Law, Vol. 354. New York, 1931.

Heitsch, E. *Die griechischen Dichterfragmente der römischen Kaiserzeit*, Vol. 1. Abh. Gött., Vol. 49. Göttingen, 1961.

Hendy, M.F. *Studies in the Byzantine Monetary Economy, c. 300-1450*. Cambridge, 1985.

Herzfeld, M. *The Poetics of Manhood: Contest and Identity in a Cretan Mountain Village*. Princeton, 1985.

(Heumann H.G. &) Seckel, E. *Heumanns Handlexikon zu den Quellen des römischen Rechts*. 9th ed. Jena, 1907.

Hobson, D.W. "Women as Property Owners in Roman Egypt." *TAPA* 113 (1983): 311-21.

—. "The Impact of Law on Village Life in Roman Egypt." In *Law, Politics and Society in the Ancient Mediterranean World*, edited by B. Halpern & D.W. Hobson (Sheffield, 1993): 193-219.

Hoogendijk, F.A.J. & P. van Minnen. "Drei Kaiserbriefe Gordians III. an die Bürger von Antinoopolis." *Tyche* 2 (1987): 41-74.

Horn, R.C. *The Use of the Subjunctive and Optative Moods in the Non-literary Papyri*. Philadelphia, 1926.

Hornickel, O. *Ehren- und Rangprädikate in den Papyrusurkunden. Ein Beitrag zum römischen und byzantinischen Titelwesen*. Giessen, 1930.

Jones, A.H.M. *The Later Roman Empire: A Social, Economic and Administrative Survey*. 3 Vols. Oxford, 1964.

Kassel, R. & C. Austin. *Poetae Comici Graeci*, Vol. 5. Berlin, 1986.

Keenan, J.G. "The Names Flavius and Aurelius as Status Designations in Later Roman Egypt." *ZPE* 11 (1973): 33-63 and 13 (1974): 283-304.

—. "On Law and Society in Late Roman Egypt." *ZPE* 17 (1975): 237-50.

—. "Aurelius Phoibammon, Son of Triadelphus: A Byzantine Egyptian Land Entrepreneur." *BASP* 17 (1980): 145-54.

—. "An Afterthought on the Names Flavius and Aurelius." *ZPE* 53 (1983): 245-50.

—. "The Aphrodito Papyri and Village Life in Byzantine Egypt." *BSAC* 26 (1984): 51-63.

—. "Aurelius Apollos and the Aphrodite Village Élite."*Atti del XVII congresso internazionale di papirologia*, Vol. 3 (Naples, 1984): 957-63.

—. "Notes on Absentee Landlordism at Aphrodito." *BASP* 22 (1985): 137-69.

—. "Village Shepherds and Social Tension in Byzantine Egypt." *YCS* 28 (1985): 245-59.

—. "On Languages and Literacy in Byzantine Aphrodito." *Proceedings of the XVIII International Congress of Papyrology*, edited by B.G. Mandilaras, Vol. 2 (Athens, 1988): 161-67.

——. "On the Cairo Maspero Papyri." *Proceedings of the XIXth International Congress of Papyrology*, Vol. 1 (Cairo, 1992): 85-94.

——. "Papyrology and Byzantine Historiography." *Alpha to Omega: Studies in Honor of George John Szemler on his Sixty-Fifth Birthday*, edited by W.J. Cherf (Chicago, 1993): 111-22.

Koenen, L. *Eine ptolemäische Königurkunde* (P.Kroll.). Klassisch-Philologische Studien, Vol. 19. Wiesbaden, 1957.

Koenen, L. & C. Römer. *Der Kölner Mani-Kodex. Über das Werden seines Leibes. Kritische Edition*. Pap. Colon., Vol. 14. Opladen, 1988.

Krause, M. "Ein Fall friedensrichtlicher Tätigkeit im ersten Jahrzehnt des 7. Jhdts. im Oberägypten." *RdÉ* 24 (1972): 101-07.

Kreller, H. "Διάδοχοc und κληρονόμοc." In *Papyri und Altertumswissenschaft*, edited by W. Otto & L. Wenger. Münch. Beitr., Vol. 19 (Munich, 1934): 233-42.

Kuehn, C.A. "A New Papyrus of a Dioscorian Poem and Marriage Contract." *ZPE* 97 (1993): 103-15.

Kuehn, Th. *Law, Family, and Women: Towards a Legal Anthropology of Renaissance Italy*. Chicago, 1991.

Lefebvre, G. *Fragments d'un manuscrit de Ménandre*. Cairo, 1907.

Liebs, D. "Das Gesetz im spätrömischen Recht." In *Das Gesetz in Spätantike und frühem Mittelalter: 4. Symposion der Kommission "Die Funktion des Gesetzes in Geschichte und Gegenwart,"* edited by W. Sellert. Abh. Gött., Vol. 196 (Göttingen, 1992): 11-27.

MacCoull, L.S.B. "Notes on the Social Structure of Late Antique Aphrodito." *BSAC* 26 (1984): 65-77.

——. *Dioscorus of Aphrodito: His Work and His World*. Berkeley, 1988.

——. "More Missing Pieces of the Dioscorus Archive." *Actes du IVe Congrès Copte*, edited by M. Rassart-Debergh & J. Ries, Vol. 2. Publications de l'Institut Orientaliste de Louvain, Vol. 41 (Louvain-la-Neuve, 1992): 104-10.

Mandilaras, B.G. *The Verb in the Greek Non-literary Papyri*. Athens, 1973.

Maresch, K. *Nomismata und Nomismatia. Beiträge zur Geldgeschichte Ägyptens im 6. Jahrhundert n.Chr.* Pap. Colon., Vol. 21. Opladen, 1994.

——. & P.J. Sijpesteijn. "P.Lond. III 1077 descr.: metrologische Tabellen." *ZPE* 99 (1993): 57-72.

Mayser, E. *Grammatik der griechischen Papyri aus der Ptolemäerzeit.* 5 Vols. Berlin, 1926-38.

—, & H. Schmoll. *Grammatik der griechischen Papyri aus der Ptolemäerzeit,* Vol. 1.1. 2d ed. Berlin, 1970.

Minnen, P. van. "Isocrates and Menander in Late Antique Perspective." *GRBS* 30 (1992): 87-98.

Modrzejewski, J. "Private Arbitration in the Law of Greco-Roman Egypt." *JJP* 6 (1952): 239-56.

Nörr, D. "Zur Reskriptenpraxis in der hohen Prinzipatszeit." *ZSS* 98 (1981): 1-46.

Porter, S.E. *Verbal Aspect in the Greek of the New Testament with Reference to Tense and Mood.* Studies in Biblical Greek, Vol. 1. New York, 1989.

Rathbone, D.W. "Villages, Land and Population in Graeco-Roman Egypt." *PCPhS* 36 (1990): 103-42.

Rémondon, R. "Les contradictions de la société égyptienne à l'époque byzantine." *JJP* 18 (1974): 17-32.

Robert, L. "La titulature de Nicée et de Nicomédie: la gloire et la haine." *HSCP* 81 (1977): 1-39.

Rouillard, G. *L'administration civile de l'Égypte byzantine.* 2d ed. Paris, 1928.

San Nicolò, M. *Vocabularium Codicis Iustiniani,* 2 Vols. Prague, 1923-1925.

Schiller, A.A. "The Budge Papyrus of Columbia University." *JARCE* 7 (1968): 79-118.

—. "The Courts Are No More." *Studi in onore di Edoardo Volterra,* Vol. 1 (Milan, 1969): 469-502.

Schnebel, M. *Die Landwirtschaft im hellenistischen Ägypten.* Münch. Beitr., Vol. 7. Munich, 1925.

Schönbauer, E. "Pragmatica Sanctio." *FF* 35 (1961): 179-83.

Seidl, E. "Die Jurispridenz ägyptischer Provinzialrichter byzantinischer Zeit." In *Festschrift für Ernst Rabel,* edited by W. Kunkel & H.J. Wolff, Vol. 2 (Tübingen, 1954): 235-61.

Sijpesteijn, P.J. "The meaning of ἤτοι in the papyri." *ZPE* 90 (1992): 241-50.

Simon, D. *Untersuchungen zur Praxis der Stipulationsklausel*. Münch. Beitr., Vol. 48. Munich, 1964.

—. *Untersuchungen zum justinianischen Zivilprozess*. Münch. Beitr., Vol. 54. Munich, 1969.

—. "Zur Zivilgerichtsbarkeit im spätbyzantinischen Ägypten." *RIDA* III 18 (1971): 623-57.

Smelik, K.A.D. & E.A. Hemelrijk. "'Who Knows Not What Monsters Demented Egypt Worships? Opinions on Egyptian Animal Worship in Antiquity as Part of the Ancient Conception of Egypt." *ANRW* II 17.4 (1984): 1852-2000.

Steinwenter, A. *Studien zu den koptischen Rechtsurkunden aus Oberägypten*. Stud. Pal., Vol. 19. Leipzig, 1920.

—. *Die Streitbeendigung durch Urteil, Schiedsspruch und Vergleich nach griechischem Rechte*. Münch. Beitr., Vol. 8. Munich, 1925.

—. "Das byzantinische Dialysis-Formular." *Studi in memoria di Aldo Albertoni*, edited by P. Ciapessoni, Vol. 1 (Padua, 1935): 73-97.

—. *Das Recht der koptischen Urkunden*. Handbuch der Altertumswissenschaft X 4.2. Munich, 1955.

Sturm, F. *Stipulatio Aquiliana. Textgestalt und Tragweite der aquilianischen Ausgleichsquittung im klassischen römischen Recht*. Münch. Beitr., Vol. 59. Munich, 1972.

Tabachovitz, D. *Études sur le grec de la basse époque*. Skrifter utgivna av K. Humanistiska Vetenskapssamfundet i Uppsala, Vol. 36.3. Uppsala, 1943.

Taubenschlag, R. *The Law of Greco-Roman Egypt in the Light of the Papyri*. 2d ed. Warsaw, 1955.

Till, W.C. *Erbrechtliche Untersuchungen aufgrund der koptischen Urkunden*. Österreichische Akademie der Wissenschaften, Sitzungsberichte, Vol. 229.2. Vienna, 1953.

Turner, E.G. "The Charioteers from Antinoe." *JHS* 93 (1973): 192-95.

—. *The Terms Recto and Verso. The Anatomy of the Papyrus Roll*. Pap. Brux., Vol. 16. Brussels, 1978.

Wenger, L. *Die Stellvertretung im Rechte der Papyri*. Leipzig, 1906.

West, L.C. & A.C. Johnson. *Currency in Roman and Byzantine Egypt*. Princeton University Studies in Papyrology, Vol. 5. Princeton, 1944.

West, M.L. *Hesiod, Works and Days. Prolegomena and Commentary*. Oxford, 1978.

Wipszycka, E. *Les ressources et les activités économiques des églises en Égypte du IVe au VIIIe siècle*. Brussels, 1972.

——. "Le degré d'alphabétisation en Égypte byzantine." *RÉAug* 30 (1984): 279-96.

Wolff, H.J. "Der byzantinische Urkundenstil Ägyptens im Lichte der Funde von Nessana und Dura." *RIDA* III 8 (1961): 115-54.

——. "Some Observations on Praxis." *Proceedings of the Twelfth International Congress of Papyrology*, edited by D.H. Samuel. ASP, Vol. 7 (Toronto, 1970): 527-35.

Worp, K.A. "Byzantine Imperial Titulature in the Greek Documentary Papyri: The Oath Formulas." *ZPE* 45 (1982): 199-223.

Ziegler, K.-H. *Das private Schiedsgericht im antiken römischen Recht*. Münch. Beitr., Vol. 58. Munich, 1971.

Zilliacus, H. *Zur Abundanz der spätgriechischen Gebrauchssprache*. Commentationes Humanarum Litterarum, Vol. 41.2. Helsinki, 1967.

Greek Index

References are to line numbers of the transcription of the Greek text unless otherwise stated. The article is omitted. For family relations see also the family tree on p. 131.

Subject Index

References are to pages in the introduction and line numbers (in *italics*) in the commentary.

Subject Index

References are to pages in the introduction and line numbers (in *italics*) in the commentary.

Plates

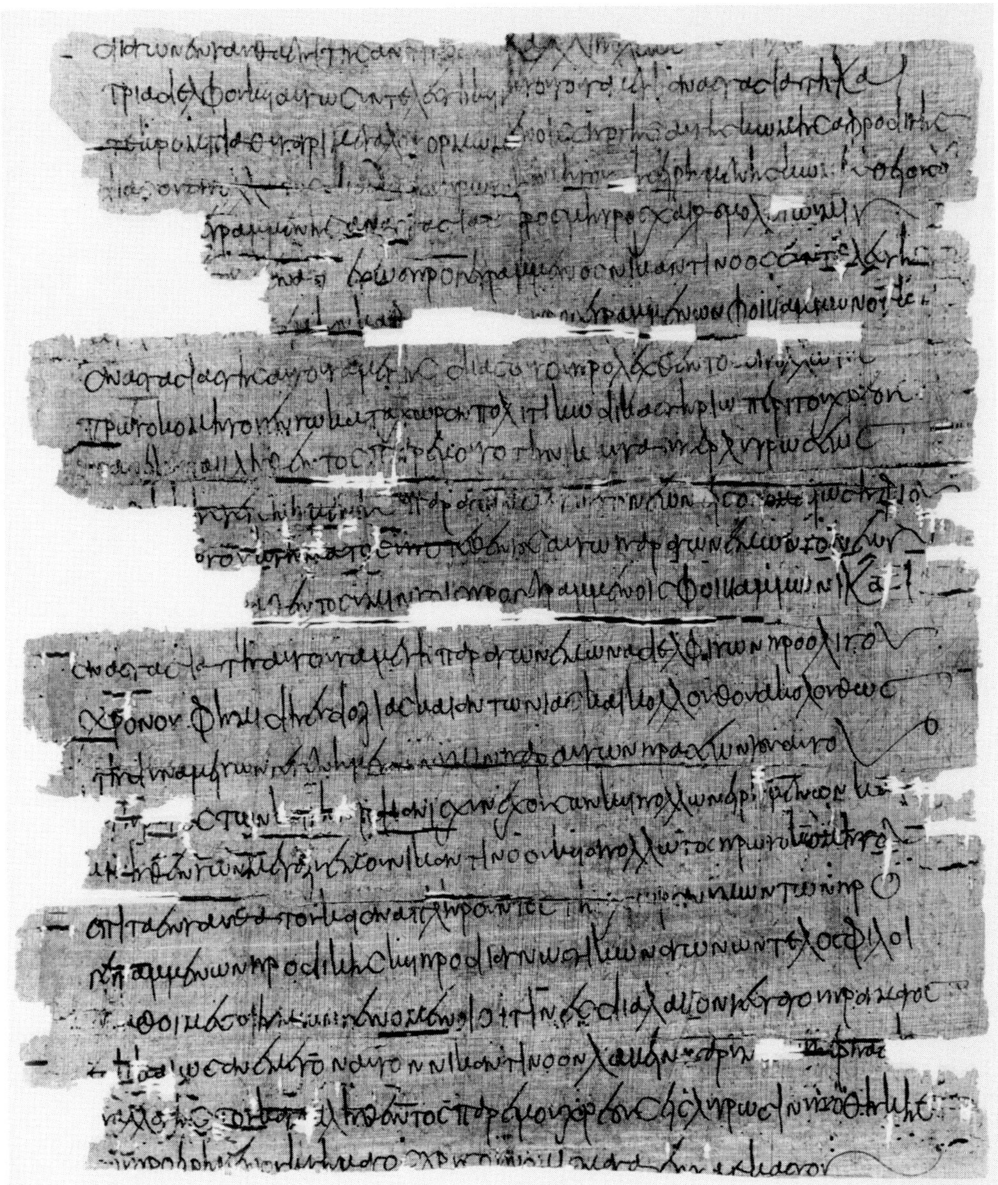

Pl. 1. Lines 1a–24

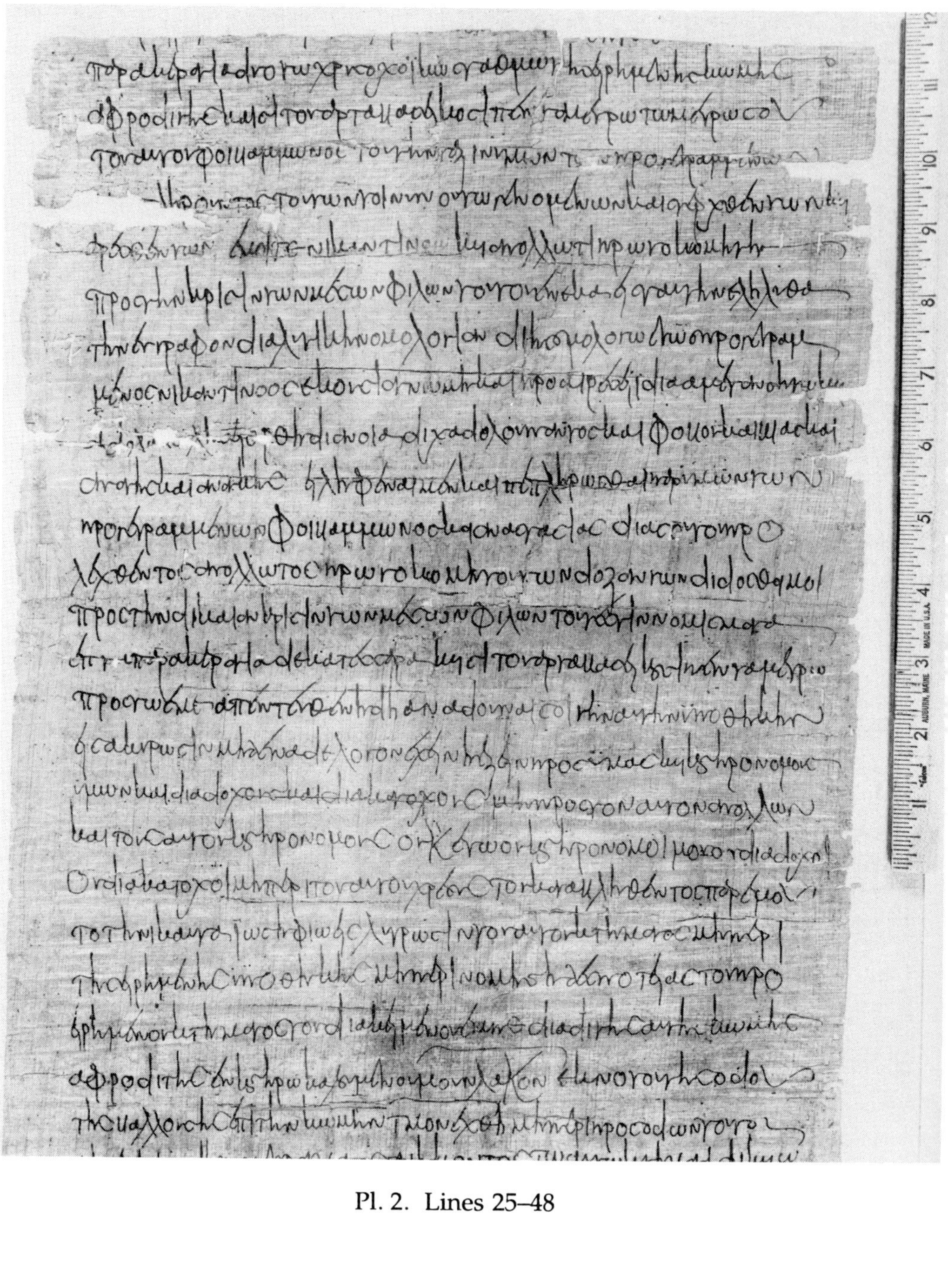

Pl. 2. Lines 25–48

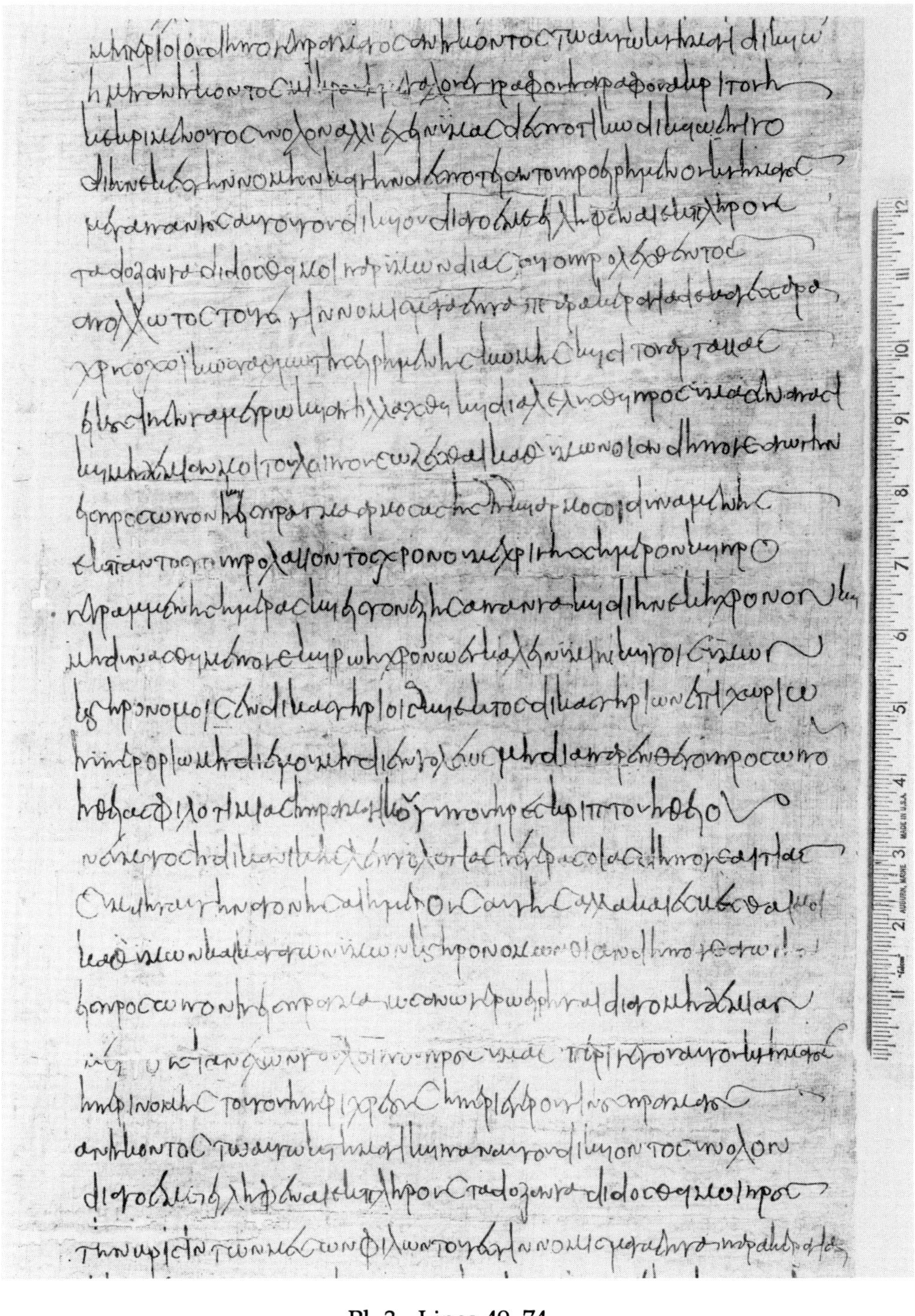

Pl. 3. Lines 49–74

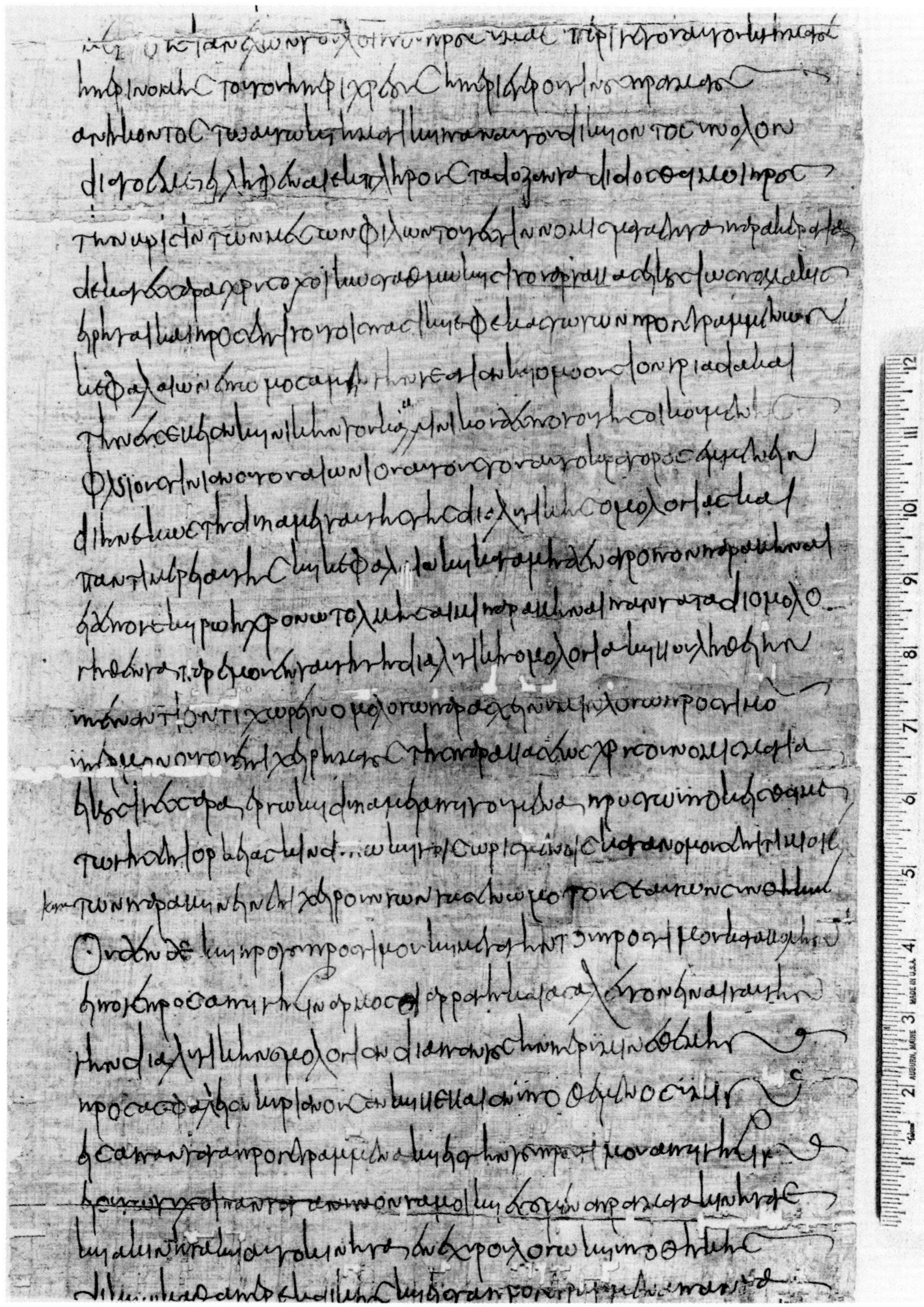

Pl. 4. Lines 70–96

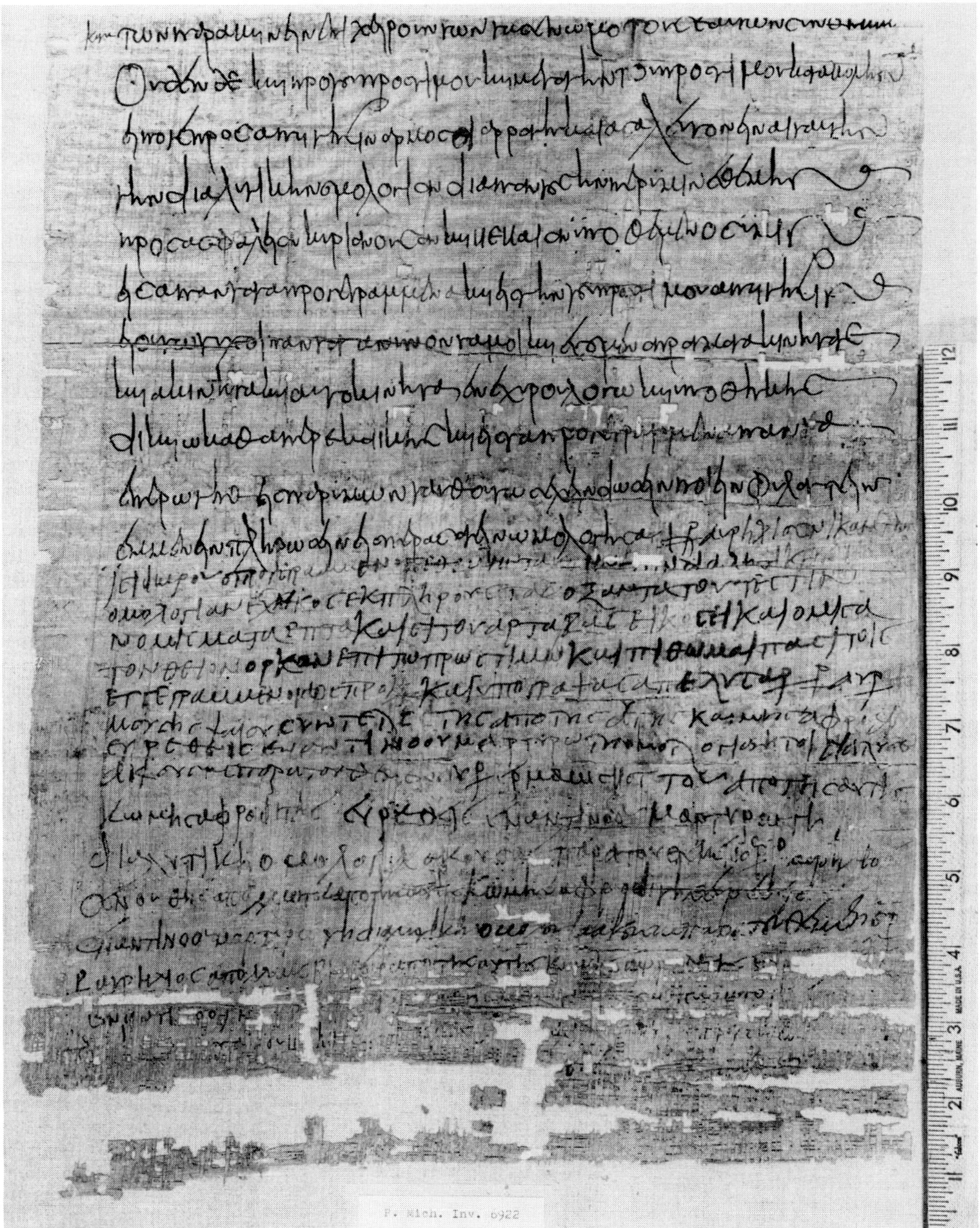

Pl. 5. Lines 88–116